Mélanie Voituriez

Little Delights in Leather

Charming Projects to Use Every Day

SCHIFFER PUBLISHING
4880 Lower Valley Road • Atglen, PA 19310

Other Schiffer Books on Related Subjects:

Tanned Leather Hand-Made Bags: Ultimate Techniques, Yoko Ganaha and Piggy Tsujioka, ISBN 978-0-7643-5612-4

Quilted Leather: Adding Texture, Dimension, and Style to Leather Crafting, Cathy Wiggins, ISBN 978-0-7643-5500-4

Inspiration Kantha: Creative Stitchery and Quilting with Asia's Ancient Technique, Anna Hergert, ISBN 978-0-7643-5357-4

Originally published as *Petits riens en cuir* by L'inédite, Paris © 2014.
Translated from the French by Omicron Language Solutions, LLC.

Library of Congress Control Number: 2019936854

Designed by Nelly Riedel
Cover design by Molly Shields
Type set in Caecilia LT Std

ISBN: 978-0-7643-5838-8
Printed in China

Published by Schiffer Publishing, Ltd.
4880 Lower Valley Road
Atglen, PA 19310
Phone: (610) 593-1777; Fax: (610) 593-2002
E-mail: Info@schifferbooks.com
Web: www.schifferbooks.com

For our complete selection of fine books on this and related subjects, please visit our website at www.schifferbooks.com. You may also write for a free catalog.

Schiffer Publishing's titles are available at special discounts for bulk purchases for sales promotions or premiums. Special editions, including personalized covers, corporate imprints, and excerpts, can be created in large quantities for special needs. For more information, contact the publisher.

We are always looking for people to write books on new and related subjects. If you have an idea for a book, please contact us at proposals@schifferbooks.com.

Sources

The leathers, fabrics, embellishments, and other accessories used in this book are from the following sources:

France Duval Stalla, for textiles, hides, accessories, leather paint, etc.
www.franceduvalstalla.com

Cuirs et Peaux, for their large choice of hides.
http://stores.ebay.fr/Cuirs-et-Peaux

Peausserie Poulain, for their very high-quality hides.
http://peausseriepoulain.com

Atelier Brunette, for their pretty printed textiles.
www.atelierbrunette.com

Stragier, for the printed cotton fabrics.
www.stragier.com

Madame Mademoiselle, for the little iron-on cats.
www.madamemademoiselle.fr

Un Oiseau sur la Branche and Shlomit Offir, for the jewelry seen throughout this book.
www.unoiseausurlabranche.com

April Eleven, for the pretty coat hook on page 25.
www.aprileleven.fr

Acknowledgments

This book is the fruit of a long, lovely, and sometimes difficult adventure; I would like to thank my little family and my friends who helped me, supported me (in every sense of the term!), and encouraged me during those intense months.

I would also like to thank France, Annabelle, Nicolas, Judith, and Frederique, suppliers of the materials that give me so much inspiration.

A special thanks to Clemence and Gi for their expert eye and patience during shooting sessions. Thank you too, pretty little Madeleine (the only part you see of her is her feet) and your mom, Stephanie, of course.

And finally, I would like to thank Nelly for her terrific work on the layout of this book.

Contents

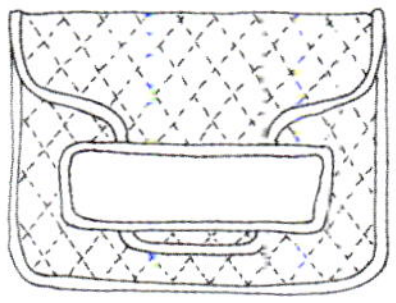

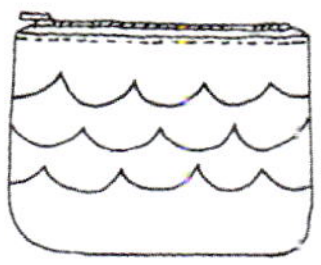

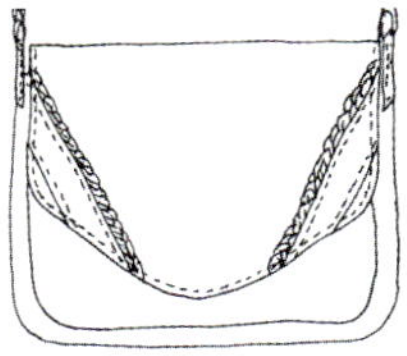

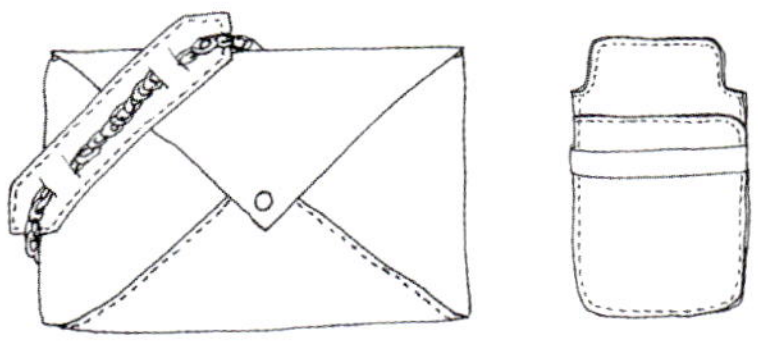

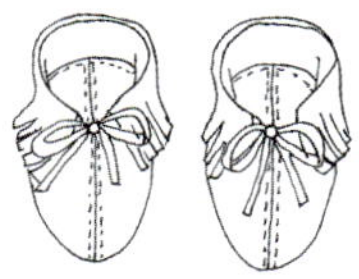

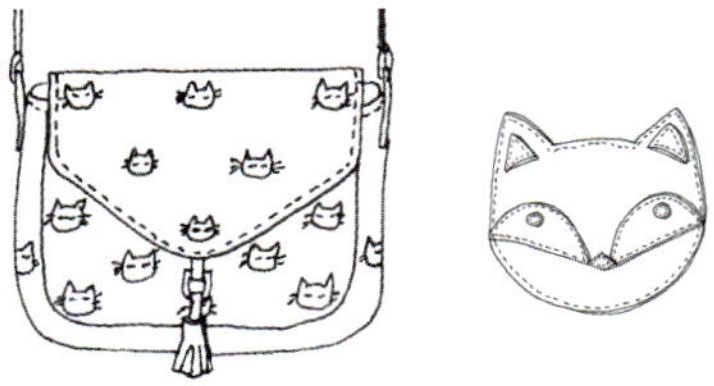

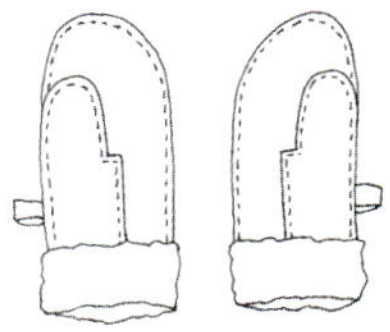

Leather Weight/Thickness Conversions

Ounces	Inches	Millimeters
2–3 oz.	1⁄32–3⁄64 in.	0.8–1.2 mm
3–4 oz.	3⁄64–1⁄16 in.	1.2–1.6 mm
4–5 oz.	1⁄16–5⁄64 in.	1.6–2.0 mm
5–6 oz.	5⁄64–3⁄32 in.	2.0–2.4 mm
6–7 oz.	3⁄32–7⁄64 in.	2.4–2.8 mm
7–8 oz.	7⁄64–1⁄8 in.	2.8–3.2 mm
8–9 oz.	1⁄8–9⁄64 in.	3.2–3.6 mm
9–10 oz.	9⁄64–5⁄32 in.	3.6–4.0 mm
10–11 oz.	5⁄32–11⁄64 in.	4.0–4.4 mm

Leather is usually measured in terms of ounces, and 1 ounce equals 1⁄64" in thickness. There is always a slight thickness variation throughout a natural hide, and so leathers are usually categorized using a range, as you see in the chart.

Introduction

My love affair with leather began a few years ago when a friend gave me some lovely remnants of leather, saying something like "You never throw anything away, so you'll find something to do with these!"

I'd never sewn leather before, and right away I loved the blend of extreme softness and strength! However, my old sewing machine was less happy about it. Because it didn't occur to me to ask anyone about sewing leather with a regular sewing machine, I spent several months using standard needles that kept breaking (odd!) and a metal presser foot that kept the leather from slipping along. What a relief when I finally learned the basics and switched to a Teflon presser foot and special needles for leather!

I'm telling you all this to explain that I've tried to write a book similar to one I would have loved to have when I was starting out: easy to carry around, not too many technical terms (in contrast with so many books about leather), and featuring attractive projects.

The projects are easy to do using a regular household sewing machine. I wondered if I should include hand-sewing techniques in the book (because they're so interesting and they allow you to work with thicker leather for superb finishing touches), but that meant a lot of additional info and a more complex learning process for beginners (the saddle-stitch isn't mastered in a day!). I therefore decided to stick to sewing thin leathers, using a machine.

My aim isn't to turn you into an expert leather craftsperson, but to help you overcome any hesitations about working with such a beautiful material. You will find that leather is soft and enjoyable to work with, and you'll soon be able to show off wonderful results!

Mélanie

Join me on my blog:
www.mespetitsriens.com
and on Instagram: melanievoituriez

Leather

Introduction

Leather has been used by people to protect themselves from cold and rain since time immemorial. It's a soft, strong material that can be used in all sorts of creations. Contrary to what you might think, it's easy to work with, as long as you have a few pieces of basic equipment.

What Is Leather?

Leather is tanned animal hide; tanning is a process that prevents it from rotting. Hide left in the open rots very quickly (in damp air) or gets very hard (in dry air). To be able to use it, humans had to find a way to preserve it.

The earliest tanning method consisted of coating the hide with animal fat and working it in until it became soft and rot-proof. This is "animal" tanning, and it is still in practice in the Asian steppes and the Arctic. People later discovered that tannin, a substance obtained from the bark of oak trees and several other kinds of plants, was excellent for tanning hides. This is "vegetable" tanning and it is still used today, but it takes several months to turn hide into leather. In the eighteenth century, the demand for leather grew considerably (especially for use in army equipment), and researchers started studying tanning methods scientifically. From their research came chrome tanning, using chromium salts, and today it remains the most widely used method since it's faster than vegetable tanning.

There are numerous kinds of leather, but the ones you find most often are from cows and calves, sheep and lambs, pigs, goats and kids, horses, and the deer family, including deer, moose, caribou, etc. You might also come across more "exotic" types, such as peccary (a small South American mammal), ostrich, crocodile, snake, and even certain fish!

And, of course, there is "faux leather," a term used for materials that look like leather but do not use animal skin. The projects in this book can be sewn with it, though it doesn't necessarily behave like leather.

A Super-Short Glossary

Leather's "right side," which shows the pores and had the hair of the animal, is called the **grain side**; the other side is called the **flesh side**. Unsplit leather is called **full-grain** leather. Thick hides are generally split before tanning, which means that they are thinned. The leather made from the lower nongrain layers is called **split leather**.

Nubuck is obtained when the grain surface is buffed to become velvety.

Soft leather or suede is velvety leather obtained by buffing, and most often it is made from the inner layers of leather.

Shearling is sheep or lamb leather that hasn't had the wool removed.

Pebbled leather refers to a texture embossed onto the surface.

After it's tanned, the leather will be dyed and finished. These operations affect the texture and color of the leather.

Aniline dying is a procedure that uses transparent water-based dye. It preserves the leather's characteristics and gives it a beautiful appearance. However, it is rather fragile.

Semi-aniline dying consists of applying a thin coat of lightly opaque pigments before applying the transparent aniline product. This hides small defects.

Pigment dying consists of tinting the surface of the leather with a coat of opaque pigments, which completely hides the defects (insect bites, scars, etc.), makes cleaning easier, and makes it waterproof.

Varnishing is done by buffing the leather and applying a coat of high-gloss varnish.

The Grain

As we have seen, the grain is the side that shows the pores and hair follicles and is therefore different in each animal. Here are some examples:

Taking Care of Leather

Leather is easy to keep in good condition, but it needs a little care to maintain its quality. Leather that has been varnished or dyed on the surface is less fragile than aniline, semi-aniline, or nubuck leather, but all leathers (except varnished) remain porous and have a tendency to absorb dirt and grease. So before treating leather, carefully remove any surface dust or dirt with a soft cloth. Fragile leather, such as nubuck, soft leather, suede, and aniline, can be protected with a spray, sprayed all over the surface.

Dyed leather can be nourished with a grease-based product applied with a soft cloth.

Be sure to test a small hidden area of the item first to see if the conditioning or protective product works properly with it.

Buying Leather

Leather is sold as entire hides, half hides, or cuts. With entire hides, leather is priced by the square foot or square meter. Among hides that have undergone the same treatments, the prices can vary enormously: leather is separated into categories from 1 to 4. Leather in category 1 is perfect, while leather in category 4 shows a lot of defects: scars, insect bites, tattoos, wrinkles, etc.

How to Store Your Leather

In spite of its reputation for toughness, leather is a fragile material in some ways and shouldn't be stored carelessly. Don't store it near a heat source or exposed to sunlight. If you don't have the space to stack it flat, the second best thing is to roll it, separated by color, with the grain on the outside to maintain correct tension. Wrap kraft paper around the roll to protect the leather from the light.

Pebbled lambskin

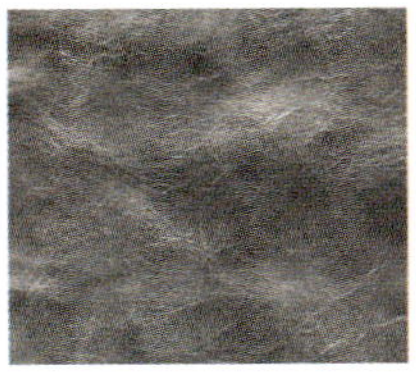
Metallic lambskin

Dyed lambskin

Dyed lambskin

Natural grain goatskin

Soft goatskin

Calfskin suede

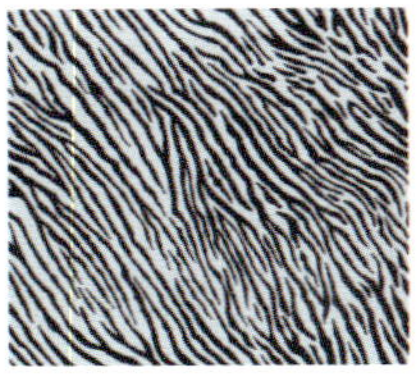
Calfskin suede

Pig suede

Calfskin

Tools and Materials

In this book we will be sewing leather by using a regular household sewing machine, which means we'll be using thin-weight leather such as lambskin, goatskin, or split skins.

These leathers sew up almost as easily as fabrics, but you do need to have some equipment. Here is a list of the tools we'll use.

- **Needles:** Whether using hand-sewing (1) or machine-sewing needles (2), it is important to use special leather needles, which have triangular tips that penetrate the leather better. For supple, thin leather, use a size 14/90 needle; for thicker leather, use a size 16/100 or even slightly thicker. Stock up so you have a handy supply of different-sized needles.
- **Thread:** For sewing leather, it is typically recommended to use waxed linen thread (3). The only problem is that it doesn't thread through household sewing machines, so we'll be using cotton thread or synthetic thread meant for thick fabrics (4).
- **Teflon presser foot** (5)**:** This is indispensible for sewing leather with a machine! It isn't usually supplied as standard with the machine, so you will likely have to buy one.
- **Silver leather-marking pen** (6)**:** Ideal for tracing your pattern directly onto the leather. The marks are removable.
- **Scissors for leather** (7)**:** You can use ordinary fabric scissors, but go for a good brand that's robust and comfortable to use. Special scissors intended for leather are available in stores; they have adjustable blades that can be set according to the thickness of the leather. Be careful: when cutting leather with scissors, always keep the scissors at the same angle in relation to the leather.
- **Rotary cutter and utility knife** (8)**:** Ideal for cutting leather that isn't too thick
- **Leather punch** (9)**:** With different-sized punches for making holes before adding snap fasteners or rivets. To keep the punches from getting blunt, it's best to slip a piece of cardboard under the leather you are punching.
- **Beeswax** (10)**:** In hand sewing this is used to wax the thread to make it stiffer and easier to sew.
- **Mallet** (11)**:** For hitting the rivet and snap fastener tools and for flattening leather
- **Leather glue:** Sometimes you can glue the pieces of leather together before sewing them. Use leatherwork glue that becomes supple and transparent when dry.
- **Wooden ruler:** For marking straight lines on the leather
- **Cutting board:** To protect your work surface when you use a mallet, hole punch, or knife
- **Masking tape** (12) **and clothespins** (13)**:** For holding the leather in place without leaving pinholes in it
- **Thread cutter:** Small scissors for snipping off the ends of the thread
- **Clothing iron:** Useful for thermoadhesive patches or iron-on transfers. You should never use the iron directly on the leather; place a piece of cloth or parchment paper between the leather and the iron.
- **Thermoadhesive patches for leather:** These are ironed onto the back side of thin leather to reinforce it.

Some tools are optional, but they can certainly come in handy!

- **Edge beveler** (14)**:** Used to cut the edges of the leather at an angle to make them thinner and easier to sew
- **Slicker** (15)**:** This is a wooden or nylon tool used to burnish the leather, to get rid of air bubbles when gluing, and to mark creases. Also called a burnisher.
- **Awl** (16)**:** For piercing leather
- **Spacer** (17)**:** Useful for marking evenly spaced stitching points when hand sewing

(4)
(13)
(10)
MERCHANT & MILLS
TAILOR'S
BEESWAX
J. WENZEL
(5)
(1)
(2)
(3)
(12)
(17)
(8)
(6)
(14)
(15)
(16)
(11)
C.S. OSBORNE & CO.
(7)
(9)

Techniques

Machine Sewing
Contrary to popular belief, leather sews up very well on a machine, as long as you take certain precautions: tightly spaced stitches weaken the leather and can cause tearing, so when you set your machine, choose a minimum stitch length of ⅛".

Before starting on an important piece of work, do some tests on scraps to make sure your machine can accommodate the different thicknesses you want to use in your project. If not, work with thinner leather.

Eyelets and rivets are usually sold in packets with the necessary tools for applying them. However, you can use multipurpose pliers with heads that can be changed to install eyelets or rivets. They are often sold in kits, with heads to match different eyelet and rivet sizes. The pliers are more expensive but make the task much easier. Be careful: before making a hole for studs, eyelets, or rivets, do a test on a scrap first to make sure the hole size is correct.

Rivets
A rivet is a metal attachment used to securely join pieces of leather. It is made up of a male part and a female part. There are several diameters and lengths available in stores. To make sure you're choosing the correct length, remember that the male part should exceed the leather thickness by 2 or 3 millimeters; that is, about ⅛".

Eyelets
An eyelet is a metal ring that is used to reinforce a hole punched in leather. Like rivets, eyelets consist of a male and a female part; the male part should exceed the thickness of the leather by 2 or 3 millimeters, approximately ⅛".

Studs

Studs are small, round metal accessories composed of two pieces. They are very easy to place and are ideal as fastening systems for bags, purses, and wallets.

Tools needed: hole punch, screwdriver, and knife

- Use the hole punch to make a hole that corresponds to the diameter of the male part of the stud (1).
- Insert the screw into the hole—it should come out on the right side of the leather (2).
- Place the stud on the screw and screw it on, using the screwdriver (3).
- For the corresponding hole (on the flap, for example), use the hole punch to make a hole with a diameter that matches the diameter of the stud. Using the knife, make a ⅛" slit ending at the hole, so that the stud can pass through the hole easily (4).

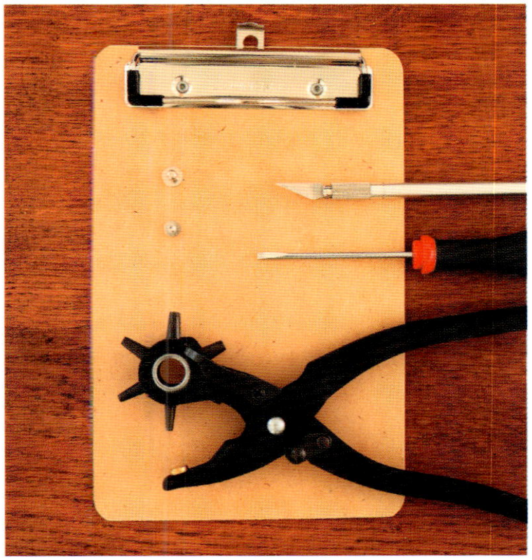

-1-

-2-

-3-

-4-

Tuck Lock Clasps

A tuck lock clasp is made up of four pieces: a tuck lock, a catch, a bar, and a backing plate.

Tools needed: a knife and a hole punch

- First of all, mark the spots where you will be setting the two parts. If we use a handbag as an example, the tuck lock part will be put on the flap, and the catch with backing plate will be put on the base of the bag. Add a small tongue (a half circle or a rectangle of leather the same size as the fastener) over the tuck lock part to make it easier to use.

- Once you have marked where the pieces are going (1), mark the tongue as well after inserting it between the flap and the metal (2).

- Using the knife, cut along the marks of the backing-plate slots. On the marks for the tuck lock, make two holes (⅛") with the hole punch. Make holes on the tongue too (3).

- Setting the tuck lock part: Slip the flap and the tongue in place, aligning all the holes. Place the metal bar, sliding the claws into the holes (4). Tighten it well and then fold the claws on the inside toward the center. Press them down with a mallet to avoid hurting yourself (5).

- Setting the backing plate: Place it on the leather, inserting the claws into the small slits (6). Place the metal plate on the inside, making sure the claws enter the slots properly, and fold them back toward the center (7).

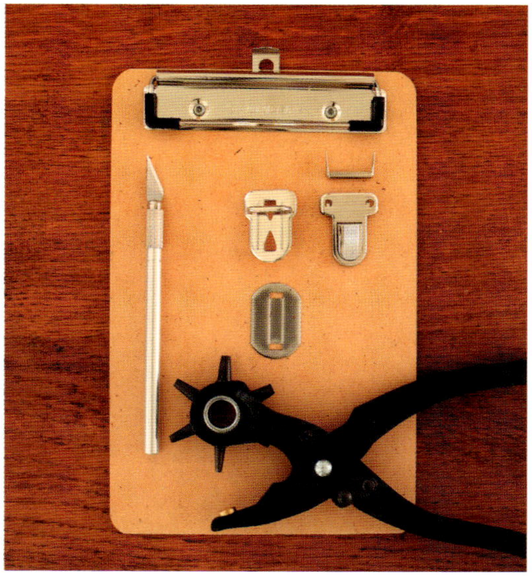

-1- -2- -3- -4- -5- -6- -7-

Magnetic Snap Fasteners

Magnetic snap fasteners are very practical and easy to set! This clasp is made of four pieces: male and female parts and two metal plates.

Tools needed: a knife and a mallet (optional)

- With a marking pen, mark the spot where the claws of the two parts are going to be inserted (1).

-1-

-2-

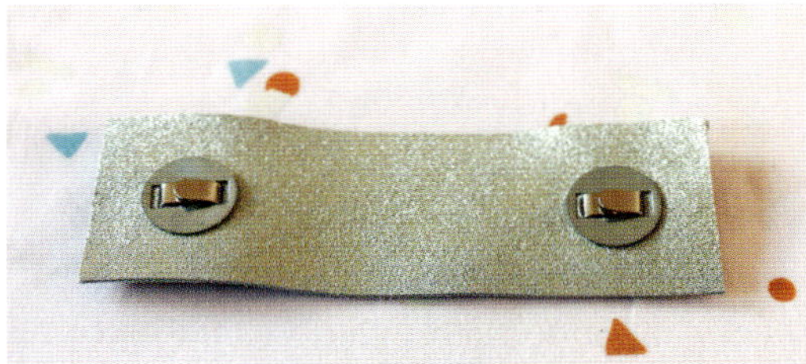

-3-

-4-

- Make slits in the leather with the knife. Make sure the claws are at the top and the bottom (and not on the sides) because these are the places that get the most wear.
- Place the buttons on their marks and slip the claws through the slits (2), and place the metal plate on the underside, making sure the claws enter the slots properly. Fold the claws toward the center, using the mallet to avoid hurting yourself (3 & 4).
- If you are attaching the fasteners to cloth, it's a good idea to place a piece of the leather between the metal plate and the cloth (6).

-5-

-6-

Making a Leather Tassel
A leather tassel is simply a rolled-up band of fringed leather.

To make one you'll need leather at the desired size—we'll use 7" × 2" in this example. Also needed are 5½" of cord, a snap hook (optional), leather glue, and a paintbrush.

- Along the underside of the leather band, trace a guide line at about ¾" from one edge. Cut fringes about 3/16" apart, stopping at the guide line (1).

- Fold your cord in half, stringing it through the the snap hook or ring if you are using one. Place the two ends of the cord on one end of the band (2). You can glue it to keep it in place, but I find the best way is to tack it down with one or two stitches (with a machine or by hand).

-1-

-2-

- Spread the glue along the part of the band that doesn't have fringes, stopping at a couple of millimeters from the fringes. Roll the band up, keeping it as tight as possible (3).

- While it's drying, you can tie a piece of ribbon or a fabric strip around it to make sure the edges stay properly adhered.

- Once it's dry, you have a pretty tassel to attach to your leather project, or to use as a key ring.

-3-

Braiding Leather

We're going to start here by braiding leather with three strips. It's a simple technique and ideal for making a pretty bracelet or a handle for a bag. When braiding, it's best to use slightly stiffer, thicker (around 5 oz. / 2 mm minimum) leather.

Here are the steps:

- In your piece of leather, cut three slits the same width, leaving a few centimeters uncut at each end (1).
- Start braiding by bringing the left strip over the center one and then the right strip over that (2).
- Now bring the left strip over the center one and pass the bottom uncut part between the strips toward the back (3).
- The bottom part of the strips will look all twisted, but not to worry—that's normal!
- Continue braiding, bringing the right strip over the center one, the left one over that, and passing the bottom uncut part through the strips toward the back (4).
- At this stage the strips are usually flat (5)! Continue to braid in this way to the end.
- Adjust the strips to make sure they are evenly spaced and properly flat (6).

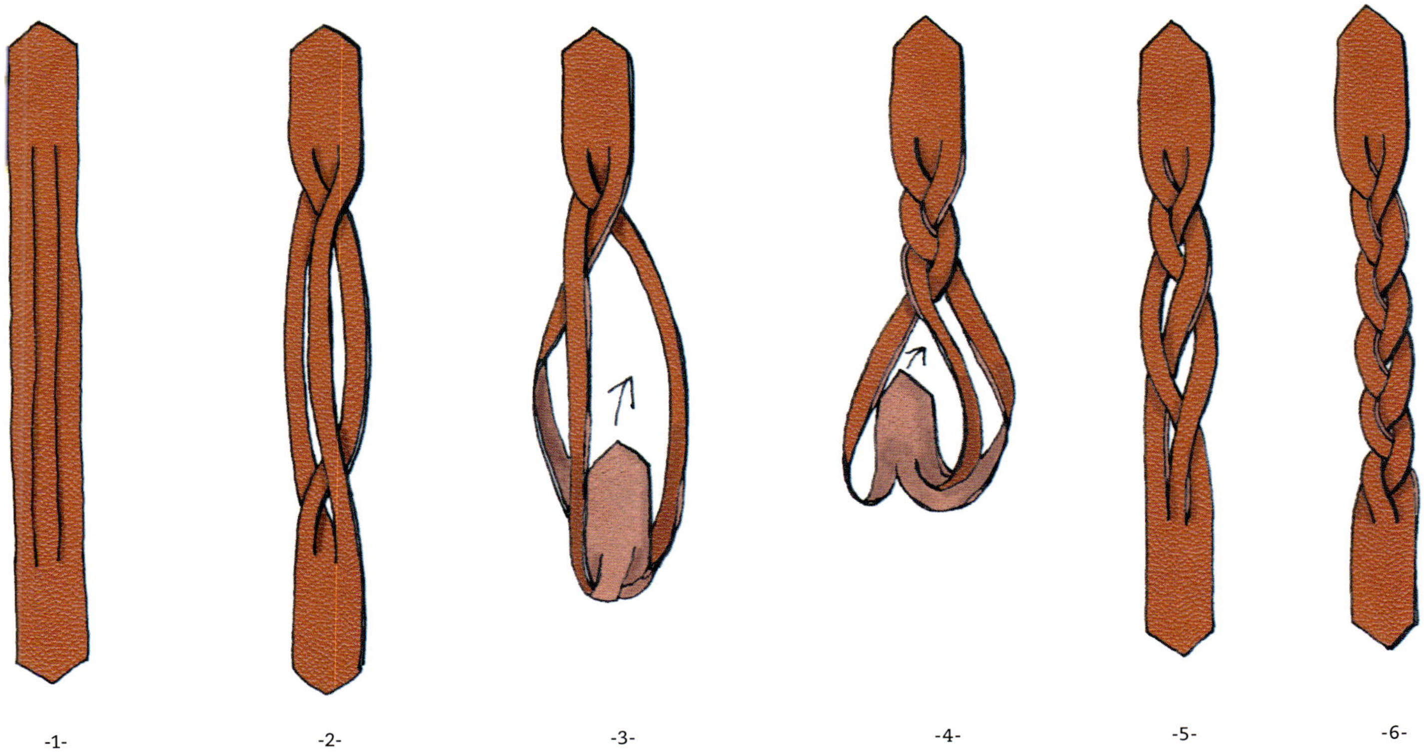

Backstitch (for Handles or Appliqué)

The backstitch is done using a round-pointed needle and waxed thread. On the right side, it will look like saddle stitch, but on the underside it will look horrible! So use backstitch only when the underside isn't going to be seen (that is, when you have a lining).

Here are the steps:

- Pierce the thicknesses of leather with your sewing machine, using a leather needle (without the thread).
- Thread your needle with yarn and make a knot at the end.
- In this example I've used a rectangle; I am going to start at the right vertical edge, so we will consider that the first hole. Hole #1 is on the top right-hand side. Insert the needle into hole #2, from the underside to the top side (1). Pull the thread through until you reach the knot.
- Make a first stitch by inserting the needle into hole #1 (2). Pull the thread through and then double the first stitch (to make it more secure) by passing the needle from hole #2 to hole #1.
- Bring the needle out by hole #3 (3) and insert it into hole #2 (4). You have just done your first backstitch!
- Continue in the same way The corners are done in the same way (5).
- When you have finished, double the last stitch (to make it more secure), insert the needle into hole #1, and make a knot on the underside (6).

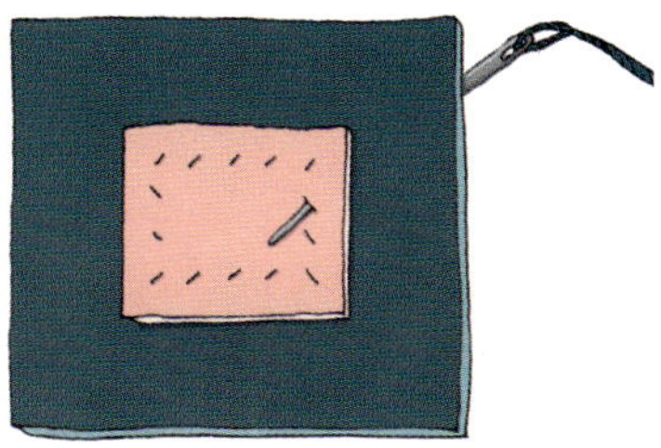

-1-

-2-

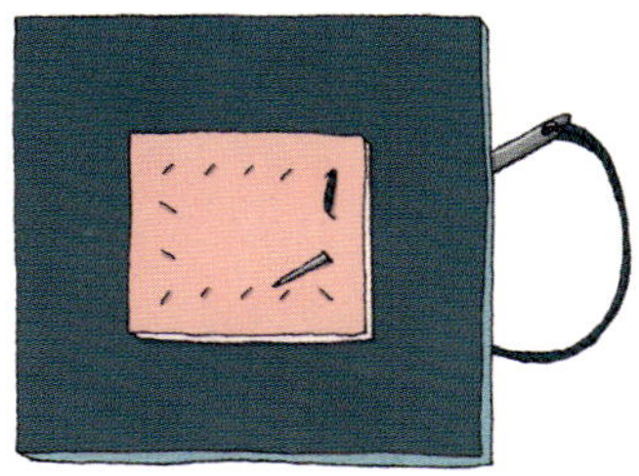

-3-

-4-

-5-

-6-

In the pages ahead, you'll find plenty to start you off on your leather creations! Remember that you will never get a result as perfect as the accessories found in fancy leather stores (unless you have an industrial sewing machine and the knowledge of a craftsperson!), but with a little patience the results will be remarkable.

Seam allowances have been taken into account in the patterns.

Tablet Case

DIFFICULTY LEVEL: ☆☆
Techniques: straight stitch (machine), applying piping, quilting
Materials: leather sewing-machine needle (size 16/100), Teflon presser foot, ruler, leather-marking pen, knife, piping presser foot
Recommended leather: thin and supple suede (goat or lambskin)
Dimensions: 7½" × 9¾" (for the large size) and 6" × 8½" (for the small size)

You'll need:

Goatskin suede (teal color): 15¾" × 23¾" (large) or 13¾" × 19¾" (small)

Cotton fabric: 15¾" × 23¾" (large) or 13¾" × 19¾" (small)

Thick fleece: 15¾" × 23¾" (large) or 13¾" × 19¾" (small)

Piping: 60"

This quilted envelope-style case will protect your tablet in style. But don't stop there—it has even more potential: by switching up colors and materials, it can be transformed into a chic evening bag!

CUTTING

- ***Back of the case:*** Cut the pattern once each out of the leather, the fleece, and the fabric.
- ***Front of the case:*** Cut the pattern once each out of the leather, the fleece, and the fabric.
- ***Wide loop:*** Cut the pattern once out of the leather and once in the fabric.

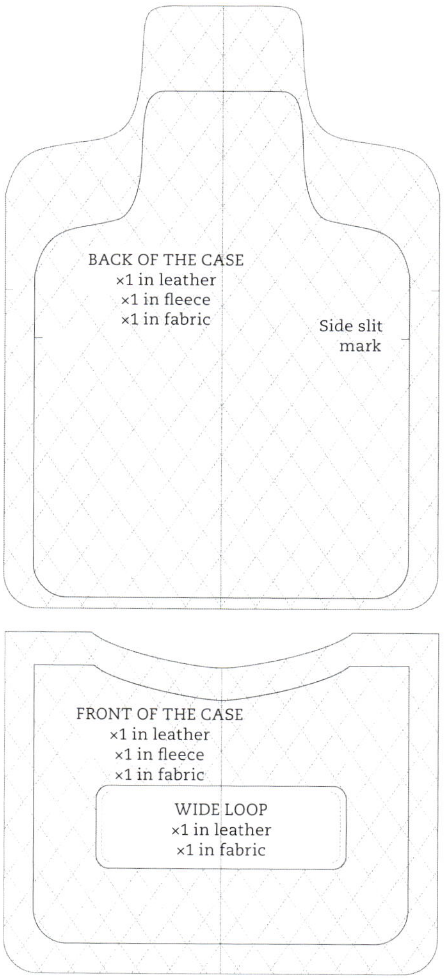

The full pattern

INSTRUCTIONS

The Quilting

- Using a leather marking pen and a ruler, mark the quilting lines on the right side of the leather (1).
- Place the pieces of leather on their fleece equivalents and tack all around the edges to keep the fleece in place (2).
- Place the Teflon presser foot on your machine and stitch along the quilting lines with a ⅛" or 3⁄16" long straight stitch (3).

The Piping

- Add the piping presser foot to your machine. Turn the case to the underside. Tack the piping all around the edge by using a large stitch, tucking one end into the other to make it neater (4). Don't hesitate to clip the piping at the curves so that the piping takes on the shape of the flap.
- Place the fabric lining on the leather right sides together. Stitch the flap between the two slit marks on the pattern, sewing along the piping; clip the curves and cut the two slits 1⁄16" from the stitches (5).
- Turn it right side out.

-1-

-2-

-3-

-4-

-5-

The Wide Loop

- Tack the piping around the wide loop, using a large stitch and tucking one end into the other to make it neater (6).

- Place the fabric lining on the leather, right sides together. Stitch all along the piping, leaving a 2" opening along one of the long sides (7).

- Clip the corners, turn it right side out, and close the opening with blind stitch.

- Place the wide loop on the front of the case, as shown on the pattern. Stitch it in place along the short sides, close to the piping as shown the drawing (8).

-6-

-7-

-8-

Finishing the Case

- Place the front of the case on the fabric lining right sides together. Stitch the top at $\frac{3}{8}$" from the edge (9).

- Clip the rounded edge and turn it right side out. Iron the fabric side to flatten the stitches.

- Place the two parts of the case right sides together, with the flap and the lining toward the top. Stitch the sides and the bottom up to the two slits on the side (10).

- Stitch the lining in the same way, leaving a 4" opening in the bottom (11).

-9-

-10-

- Clip the corners and turn the case right side out. Close the opening with blind stitch, then slip the lining into the case.

- Do some decorative edge stitching along the front of the case at about $\frac{1}{8}$" from the edge (12).

-11-

-12-

Tablet Case: Half Pattern

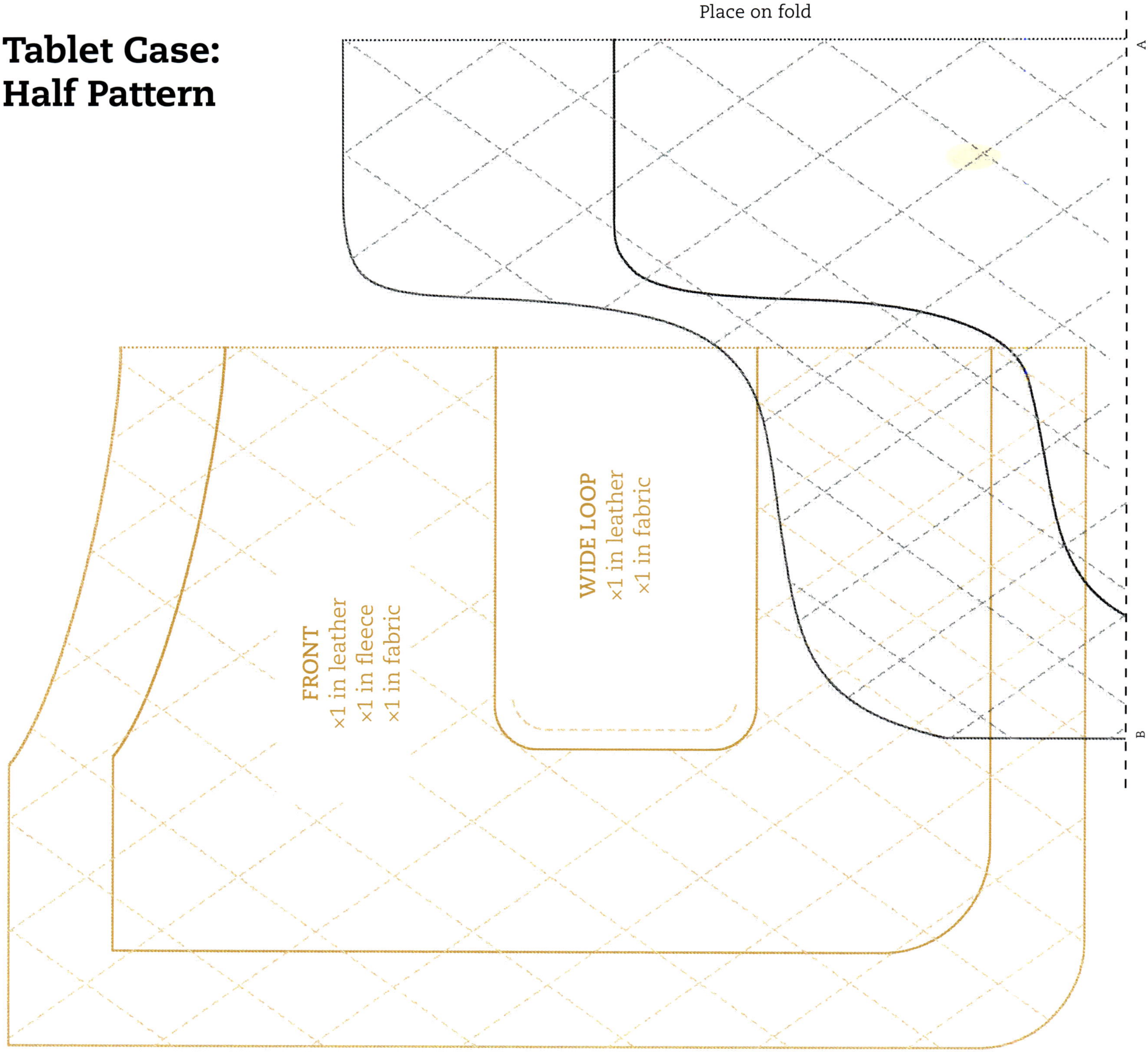

Place on fold
A
BACK AND FLAP
×1 in leather
×1 in fleece
×1 in fabric
Side slit mark
B

Braided Tote Bag and Change Purse

DIFFICULTY LEVEL: ☆☆

Techniques: straight stitch (machine), backstitch (hand), braiding

Materials: leather sewing-machine needle (size 16/100), Teflon presser foot, mallet, leather-marking pen, knife, leather needle for hand sewing, waxed thread, ruler, cutting board or mat, masking tape

Recommended leather: thin and supple, or use thicker and stiffer if you prefer, for the main part of the bag; thicker leather for the braided handles

Dimensions (without the handles): 8¾" × 11¾"

You'll need:

Natural-grain black goatskin, 5 oz. / 2 mm thick, 4" × 23¾"

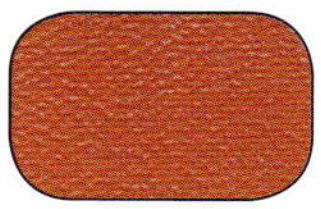

Camel-colored lambskin: 13¾" × 27½"

Cotton fabric: 13¾" × 39⅜"

Small snap hook

A matching set you can take anywhere, from a shopping spree to the office! You can make it in more or less supple leather depending on the desired effect: in thicker leather it will be stiffer; in supple leather it will be soft and squashy.

CUTTING

- ***Main part of the bag:*** Copy the pattern onto a sheet of paper 13¾" × 27½" (see the diagram below of the full pattern) and then cut it out of the leather along the cutting line for the leather.
- ***Lining:*** Cut the pattern out of the fabric along the cutting line for the fabric.
- ***Handles:*** Copy the pattern of the handles and cut it twice out of the black leather.
- ***Inside pocket:*** Cut a rectangle 11¾" × 6" out of the fabric.

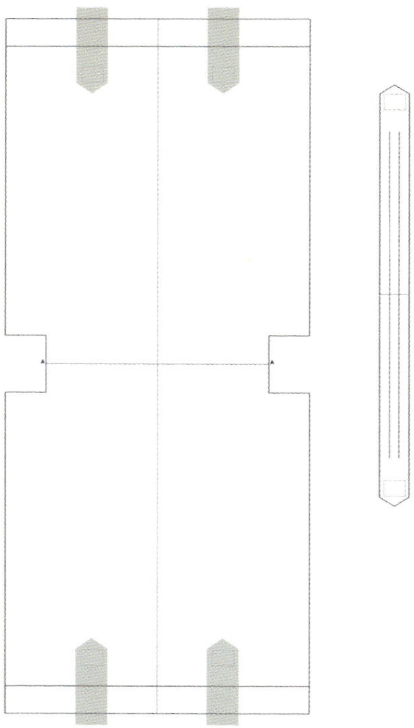

The full pattern

- ***Loop for the snap fastener:*** Cut a band 1½" × 8¾" out of the fabric.

The Handles

- On the leather for the handles, copy the reference marks (including cutting lines and sewing lines) with the leather-marking pen.
- Cut along the lines to make the slits, using a ruler and a knife (1).
- Start braiding the handles (see page 15) to the ends (2). Straighten out the braids until they are even.

-1-

-2-

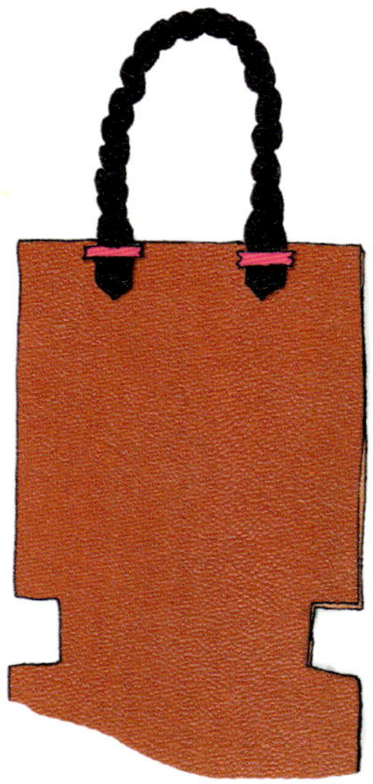

-3-

Stitching the Handles

- For this project, you can choose whether to machine or hand stitch the handles. If you sew them by hand, the thread used will be thicker and therefore the contrast will be more striking (see photo).
- In either case, fix the handles in place with masking tape (3).
- When hand stitching, if you don't have specific tools (an awl or stitch spacer wheel), you must make stitch holes in the leather along the sewing line, using your sewing machine equipped with a leather needle (without thread), setting it to a stitch size of $\frac{3}{16}$".
- Thread your needle with waxed thread and knot the end. Sew the handles by using backstitch (see page 16) (4).
- When using the machine, stitch along the sewing lines.

-4-

Lining

- Using a hot iron, fold ⅜" toward the underside on each long side of the band for the snap fastener's loop (5).

- Fold ⅜" under on one short side of the band, then fold the band in two and run the iron over it. Stitch it ¾" from the edge (6).

- Slip the band onto the snap fastener, fold 1¼", and sew it to keep the fastener in place (7).

- Fold the rectangle of fabric intended for the inside pocket in two, right sides together, and stitch three sides ⅜" from the edge, leaving an opening of 2" on one side (8). Clip the corners and then turn it right side out through the small opening.

- Run the iron over it and then close the opening with blind stitch. Do decorative edge stitching ⅛" from the edge along one short side (9).

- Place the pocket on the lining as shown in the drawing, pin, then sew it in place along three sides ⅛" from the edge. Pin on the snap-fastener band (10).

- Fold the lining in two, right sides together. Pin, then stitch the two long sides ⅜" from the edge (11).

- Open the seams with the hot iron. Fold the corners so that the side seams match up with the reference marks A. Pin and then stitch ⅜" from the edge (12).

-5-

-6-

-7-

-8-

-9-

-10-

-11-

-12-

- Fold back ⅜" to ¾" of the top of the lining to the underside and run the iron over it (13).

Finishing the Bag

- Add the Teflon presser foot and a leather needle to your machine.
- Stitch the sides and the corners in the same way as the lining.
- Slip the lining into the bag, making sure the seams match up. Place the lining edge on the outside of the bag and keep it in place with clothespins. Stitch it in place with a straight stitch ⅛" from the edge of the lining (14).

-13-

-14-

Braided Tote Bag: Quarter Pattern

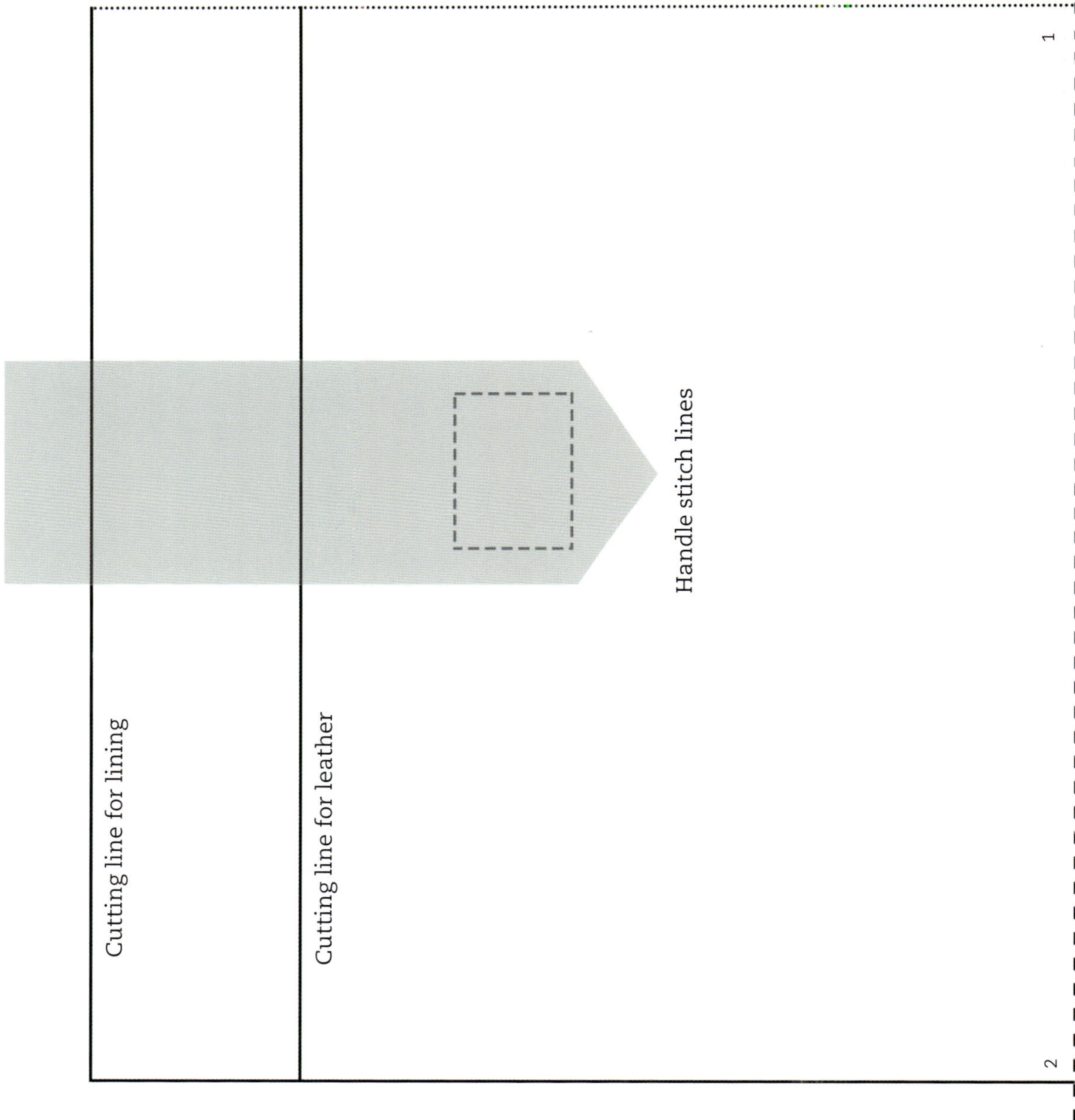

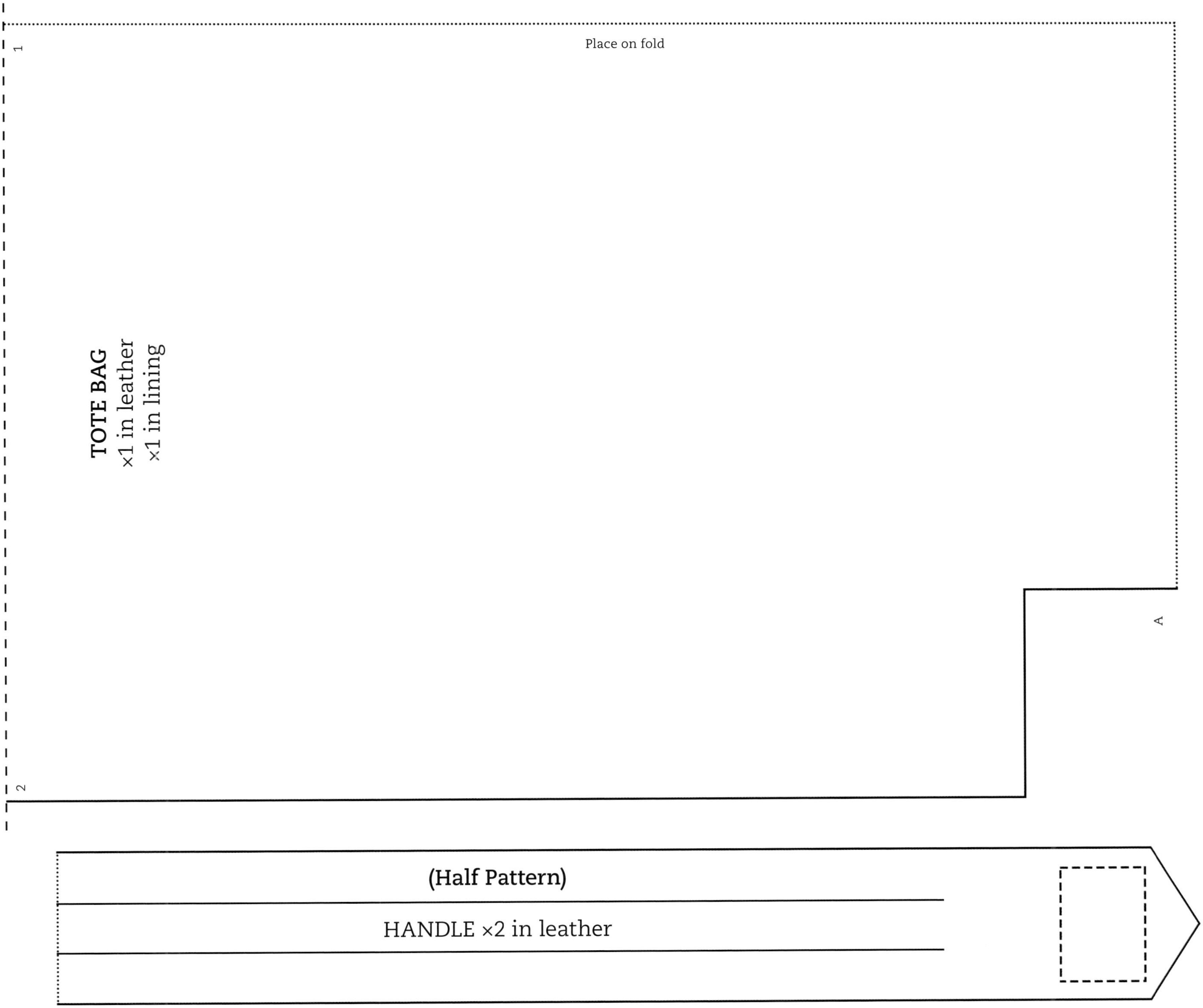
Place on fold
1
TOTE BAG
×1 in leather
×1 in lining
A
2
(Half Pattern)
HANDLE ×2 in leather

Braided Change Purse

DIFFICULTY LEVEL: ☆
Techniques: straight stitch (machine), braiding, blind stitch (by hand)
Materials: leather sewing-machine needle (size 16/100), Teflon presser foot, mallet, leather-marking pen, knife, ruler, cutting board or mat, masking tape
Recommended leather: thin leather but not too supple
Dimensions: 3" × 3¾"

You'll need:

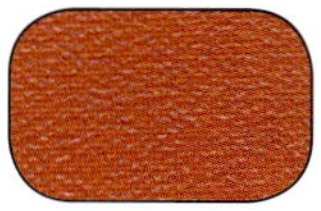

Camel-colored lambskin: 7⅞" × 6"

Cotton fabric: 7⅞" × 9¼"

Fusible interfacing for fabrics: 7⅞" × 9¼"

Magnetic snap fastener, 9/16" diameter

CUTTING
Front: Cut the pattern twice out of the fabric and once out of the interfacing.
Main part of the purse: Cut the pattern once out of the leather, once out of the fabric, and once out of the interfacing.
Loop: Cut a leather band 2" × ¼".
Braid: Cut the pattern once out of the leather.

INSTRUCTIONS

- Using the knife and ruler, make the necessary slits in the braiding leather.

- Braid (see page 15) to the end (1). Adjust the braid to give it its final form.

- Place the braided band on the main part of the purse, in the location shown on the pattern. Use masking tape to hold it in place. Fold the leather band in two (wrong sides together) to form a loop and place it, as shown in the drawing, on the main part of the purse. Stitch on the braid and the loop at 3/16" from the edge (2).

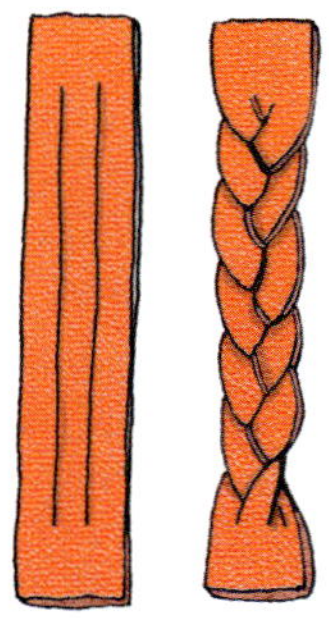

-1-

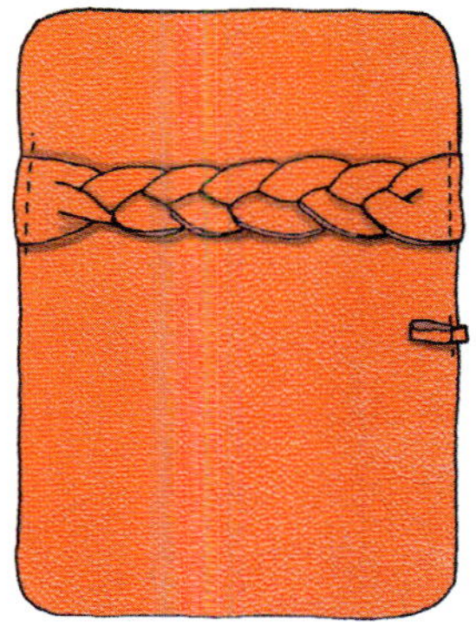

-2-

- Iron the interfacing onto the underside of the front and the lining of the main part of the purse.

- Iron a ⅜" fold on the two front parts of the fabric (3) toward the outside.

- Mark the place where the snap fasteners will go on the fabric (the female part on the front, the male part on the flap) and add a small piece of leather on the inside to reinforce them (see page 13) (4).

- Place the leather and fabric main pieces of the purse right sides together and stitch around the flap at ¼" from the edge between the two marks where the slits will be. Clip the corners and cut the slits to ¹⁄₁₆" from the seam (5). Turn the purse right side out.

- Place the front with its magnetic snap fastener on the main part of the purse, right sides together. Stitch between the two slits at ¼" from the edge (6).

- Sew the other front onto the lining in the same way (7).

- Clip the corners and then turn the leather and fabric main part right side out. Slip the lining into the interior and sew the opening with blind stitch (8).

-3-

-4-

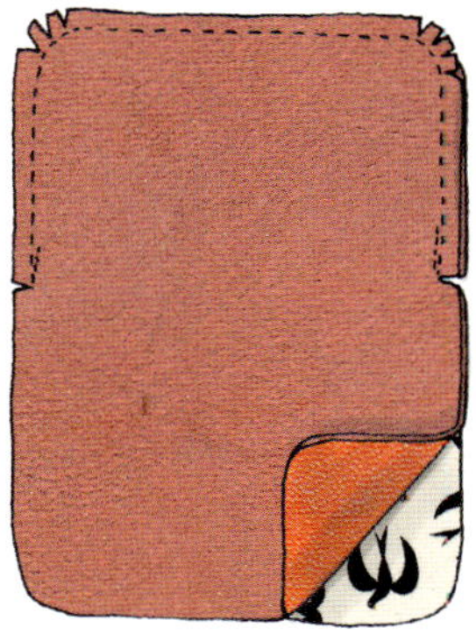

-5-

-6-

-7-

-8-

Braided Change Purse: Pattern

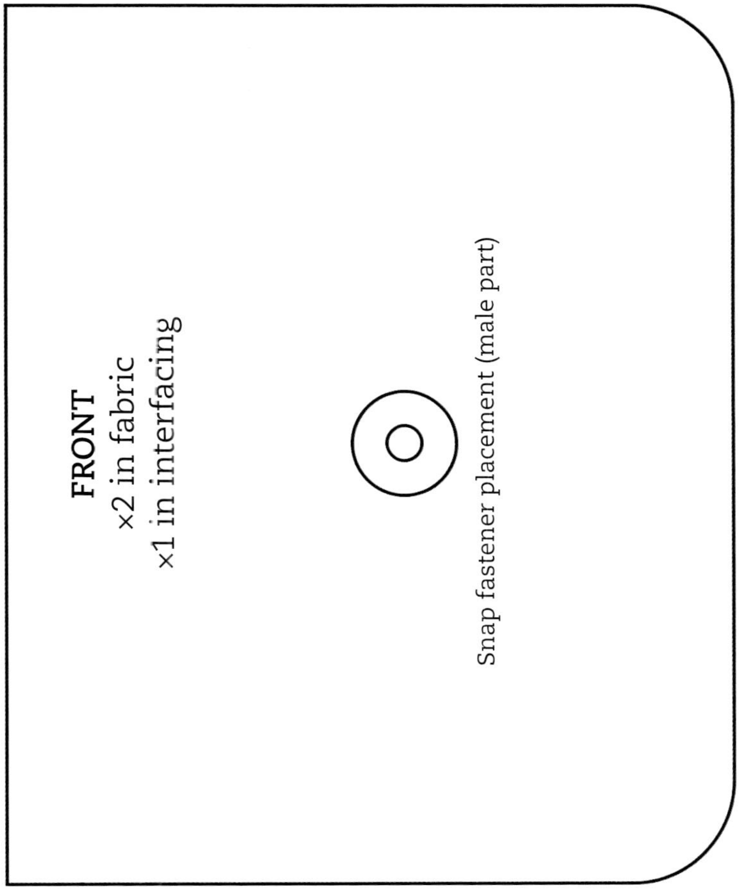

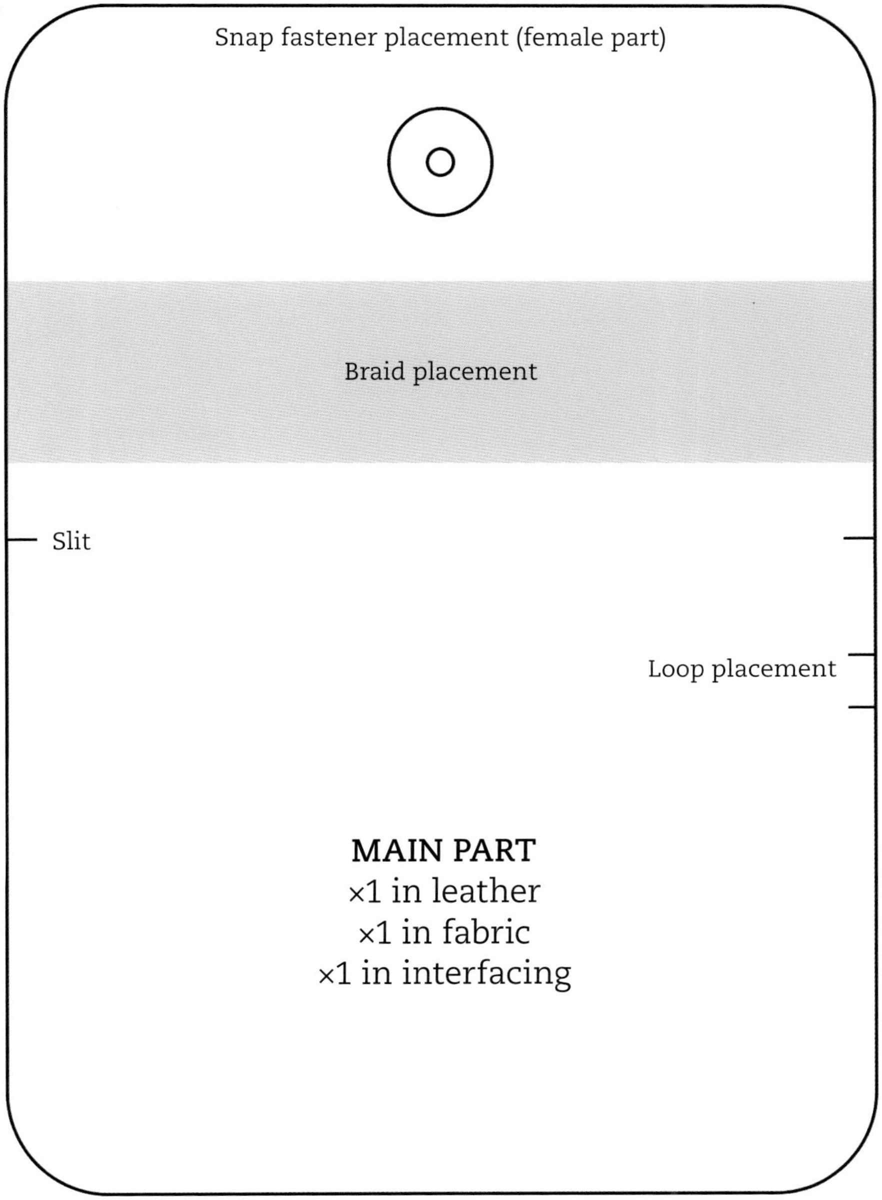

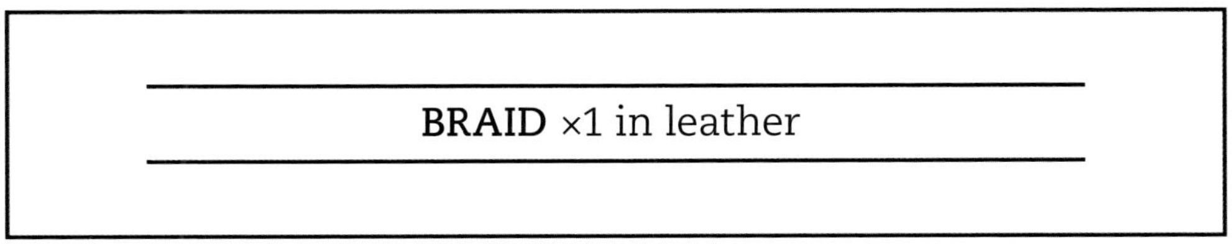

Fish-Scale-Pattern Clutch Bag

DIFFICULTY LEVEL: ☆

Materials: leather sewing-machine needle (size 14/90), Teflon presser foot, zipper

Recommended leather: fairly thin, supple leather such as nappa lambskin or suede goatskin

Dimensions: 5⅛" × 4⅛"

You'll need:

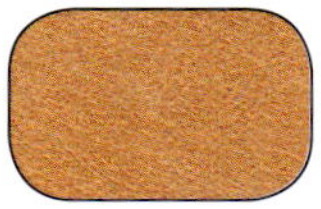 Mustard-yellow lambskin: 6" × 9½"

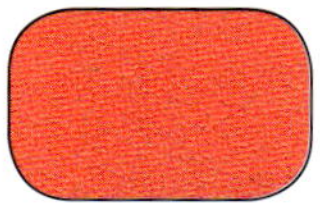 Rust-colored lambskin: 6" × 2½"

 Metallic-gold lambskin: 6" × 2½"

 Anthracite suede lambskin: 6" × 2½"

 Cotton fabric (for the inner lining): 6" × 9½"

Zipper: 6"

CUTTING

- *Main part of the bag:* Cut the pattern twice out of the mustard-yellow leather and twice out of the lining.

- *1st scale:* Cut the pattern once out of the rust-colored leather and once out of the anthracite suede.

- *2nd scale:* Cut the pattern once out of the gold leather.

A small, very easy to make clutch bag that is nevertheless very impressive! Plus, it's a great way to use up your leather scraps.

INSTRUCTIONS

- Fit a leather needle and a Teflon presser foot onto your machine. Set the gauge to straight stitch ⅛" long.
- Place the anthracite scale onto one of the main parts of the bag (use the pattern for the correct location). Use masking tape to keep it in place and stitch the upper border at ⅛" from the edge (1).
- Add on the gold- and rust-colored scales in the same way (2).
- Place the zipper along the top of the main part of the bag, right sides together, and then place one of the linings over it, underside facing outward. Fix the pieces together with paper clips. Install the foot for zippers onto your machine and stitch at ¼" from the edge (3).
- Edgestitch along the zipper stitches on the lining side and on the leather side (stitching the leather and the zipper together).
- Proceed in the same way for the other part of the zipper.
- Unzip the zipper halfway and place your work in a manner so that the two leather parts of the bag are against each other. To keep everything in place, pin the lining and use paper clips on the leather parts. Install the Teflon presser foot. Stitch all around at ⅜" from the edge and leave an opening of 2" in the lining (4).
- Clip the corners.
- Turn the bag right side out through the opening and then close the opening in blind stitch.
- Slip the lining inside the bag.

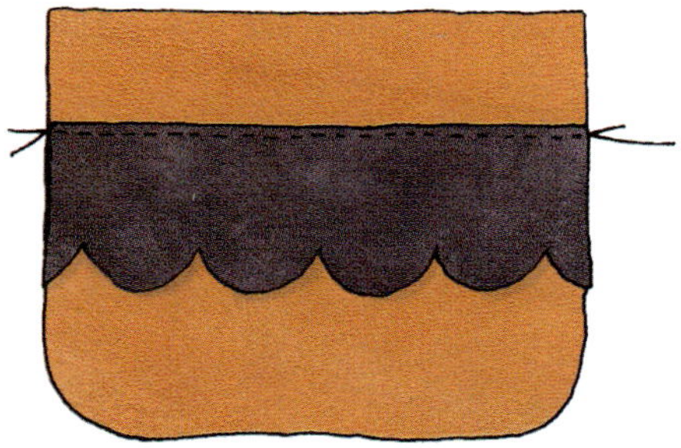

-1-

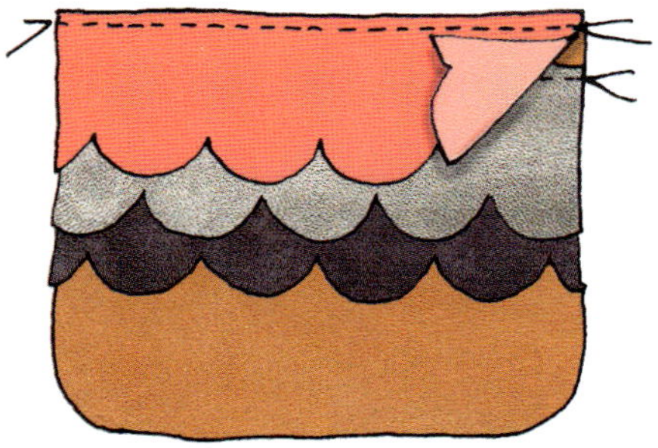

-2-

-3-

-4-

Fish-Scale-Pattern Clutch Bag: Pattern

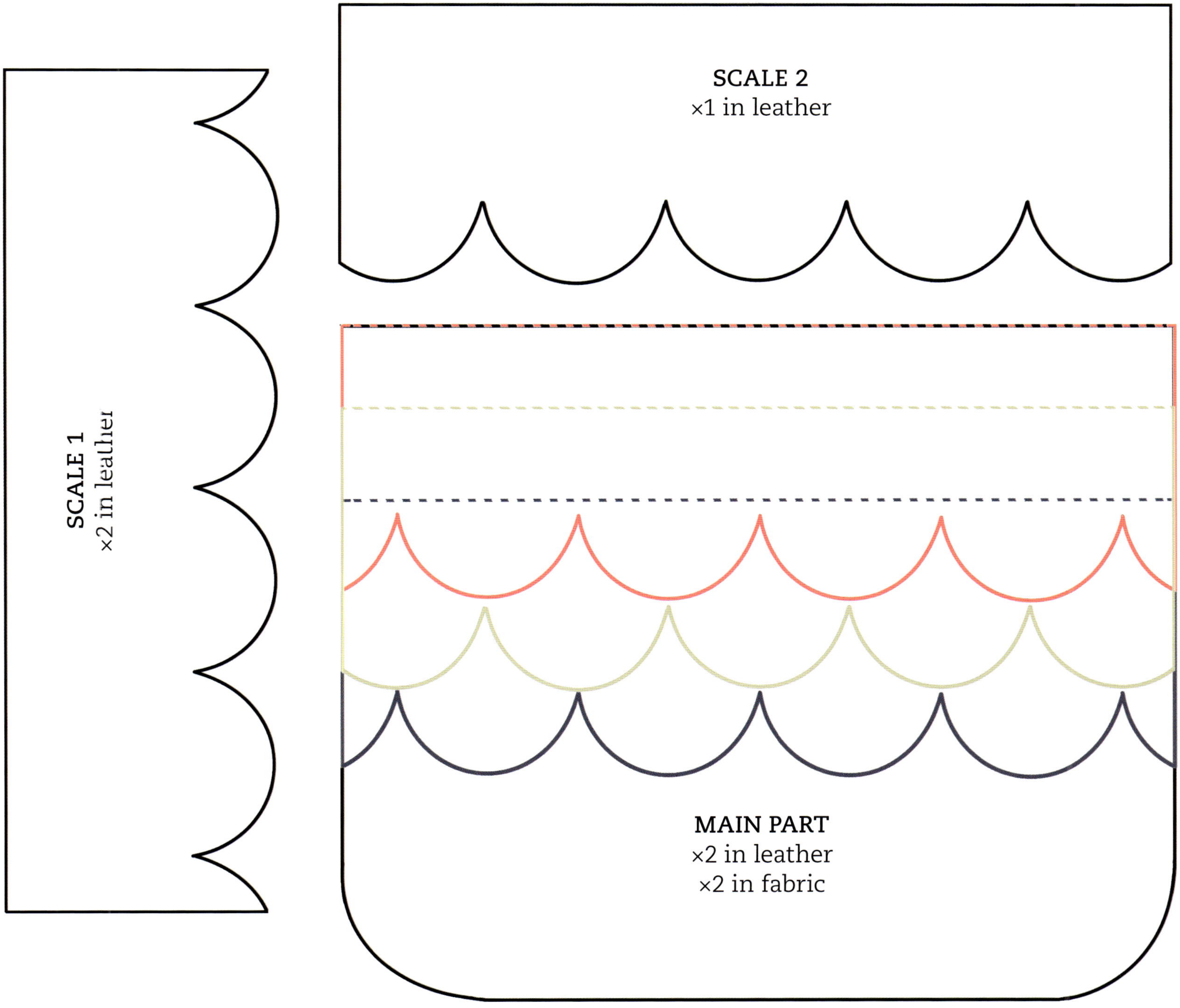

Pearlescent Shoulder Bag

DIFFICULTY LEVEL: ☆☆☆
Materials: leather sewing-machine needle, Teflon presser foot, leather glue, leather-marking pen, felt
Recommended leather: For the main part of the bag, use supple but fairly thick leather. If the leather you've chosen isn't thick enough, you can use a special leather iron-on reinforcement facing. Use very thin leather such as lambskin or suede goatskin for the appliqués.
Dimensions: 8¾" × 7" × 1¼"

You'll need:

 Pearlescent-silver suede calfskin: 23¾" × 19¾"

 Teal soft goatskin: 6" × 8"

 Cotton fabric (for the lining): 23¾" × 19¾"

 16" gold leatherette braid

Fusible interfacing for fabrics, medium weight: 11¾" × 13¾"

1 magnetic snap fastener, 11⁄16" diameter

2 D-rings, 1¼" wide

1 snap-hook chain, around 36" long

1 zipper, 6" long

A hyperfeminine, trendy shoulder bag with lots of small refined details such as the zipped pocket inside, the slit at the back, and the chain. One thing is sure: it will add a pretty touch to your look!

Frantz Funck Brentano
La Renaissance
Antoine de Saint-Exupéry
le Petit Prince

CUTTING

- ***Main part of the bag:*** Cut twice out of the silver leather. On one of the pieces, mark in the location of the slit with the leather-marking pen. Mark the location of the snap fastener on the other piece.
- ***Flap:*** Cut once out of the silver leather, once out of the fabric, and once out of the interfacing. On the leather, trace in the location of the appliquéd bands. On the fabric, trace in the location of the snap fastener.
- ***Lining:*** Cut twice out of the fabric. On one of the pieces, trace in the rectangle on the underside (the dotted lines on the pattern) with a fabric pen.
- ***Strip:*** Cut a band 21¼" × 2" in the silver leather and a band 22¾" × 2" in the fabric.
- ***Loops for attaching the shoulder strap:*** Cut two rectangles 3⅛" × 1" out of the silver leather.
- ***Appliquéd band:*** Cut twice (mirror image) out of the teal leather.
- ***Reinforcement of the inside pocket:*** Cut once out of the teal leather.
- ***Lining for the back pocket:*** Cut once out of the fabric and once out of the interfacing.
- ***Lining for the inside pocket:*** Cut a rectangle 10¼" × 8¾".
- ***Reinforcement of the back pocket:*** Cut twice out of the silver leather.

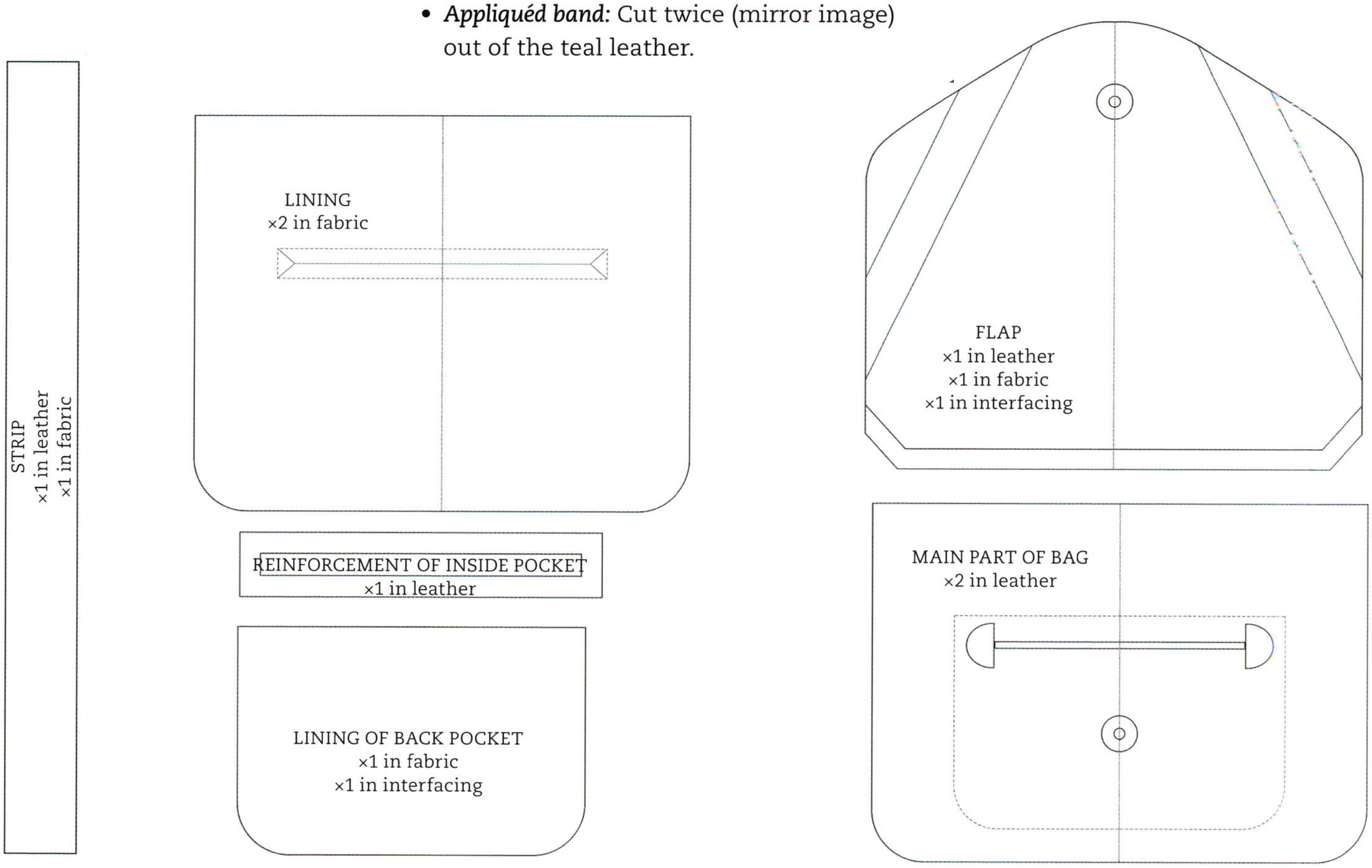

The full pattern

INSTRUCTIONS

The Flap

- Glue the braid onto the underside on the pieces of teal leather, aligning the braid along the longest side (1). Leave them to dry for a few minutes.
- Glue the bands onto the flap in the location shown in the drawing. Leave them to dry for a few minutes. Once the glue is dry, stitch along the sides of the teal leather (2).
- Iron the interfacing onto the underside of the fabric flap.
- With the iron, fold back 3/8" on the underside as shown in the drawing (3).
- Place the male part of the snap fastener in the marked location, with a small piece of reinforcing leather under it (see page 13) (4).
- Place the leather flap and its lining right sides together. Stitch 3/8" from the edge (5).
- Clip the curves and turn it right side out.
- Stitch all the way around the flap at 1/8" from the edge (6).

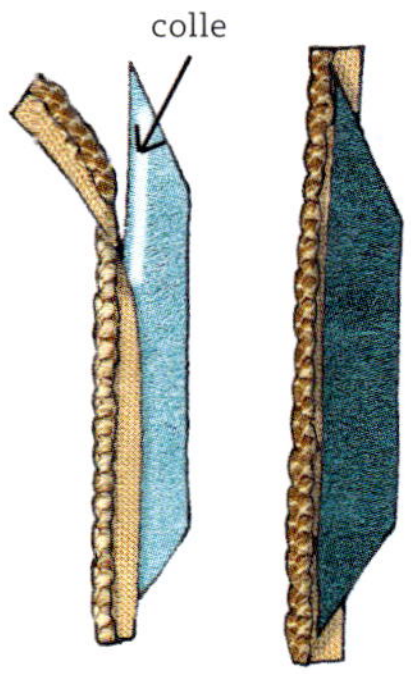

-1-

-2-

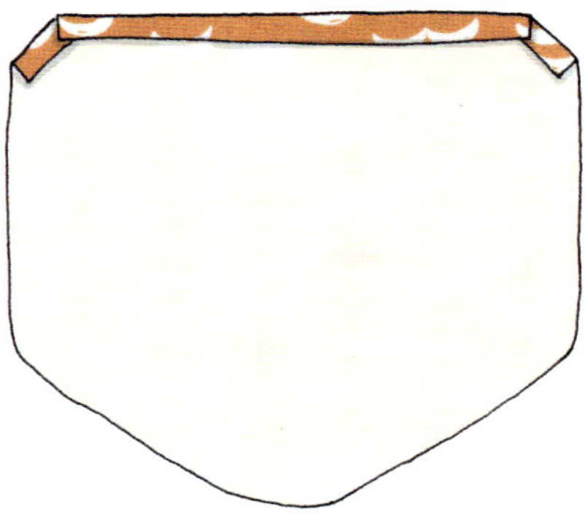

-3-

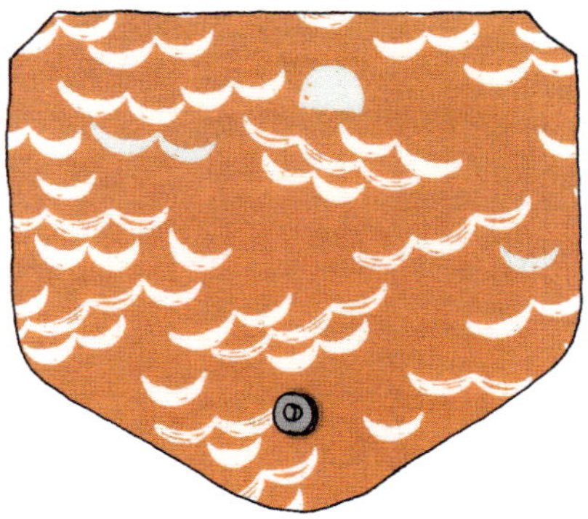

-4-

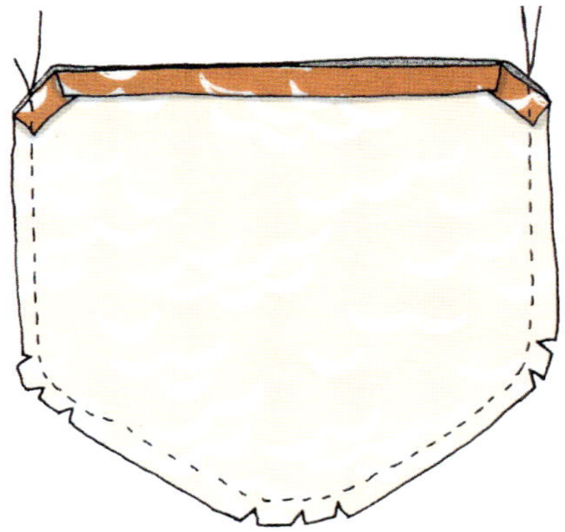

-5-

-6-

The Zipped Interior Pocket

- Take the lining piece that you have marked with the slit location for the interior pocket. Using sharp scissors, cut the central slit and the corners (gray lines on the pattern), then fold the material along the dotted lines toward the underside. Run a hot iron over them to mark the folds (7).

- Turn the lining right side up and place the teal leather reinforcement (underside of the leather against the right side of the lining). Position it so that the slit in the reinforcement matches up with the slit in the fabric. Stitch around the outside border ⅛" from the edge (8).

- On the rectangle of fabric that will be the pocket's lining, tack the zipper to the edge of one of the short sides, underside of the zipper against the right side of the material (9).

- Place it on the pocket so that the zipper is in the center of the leather reinforcement. Stitch the lower edge of the reinforcement at ⅛" from the edge (10).

- Tack the other edge of the zipper to the other edge of the pocket lining (11).

-7-

-8-

-9-

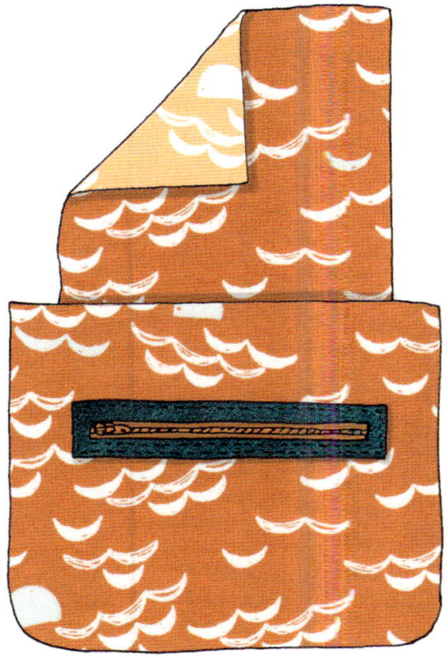

-10-

-11-

- Turn it right side out and stitch around the upper edges of the reinforcement (12).
- On the underside, stitch the sides of the pocket's lining (13).

The Lining

- Place the fabric strip right sides together on one of the bag's lining pieces; pin it evenly along the sides and the bottom and stitch it 3/8" from the edge (14).
- Assemble the other side of the strip with the other lining piece in the same way, right sides together (15).
- Fold the top edge over twice toward the underside at 3/16" and 3/8", respectively, and mark the folds by using a hot iron (16).

The Loops for the Shoulder Strap

- Slip a half ring onto each of the small rectangles for the shoulder strap loops and fold them in two. Place them on each end of the leather strip in the location shown in the drawing, and then stitch them in place (17).

-12-

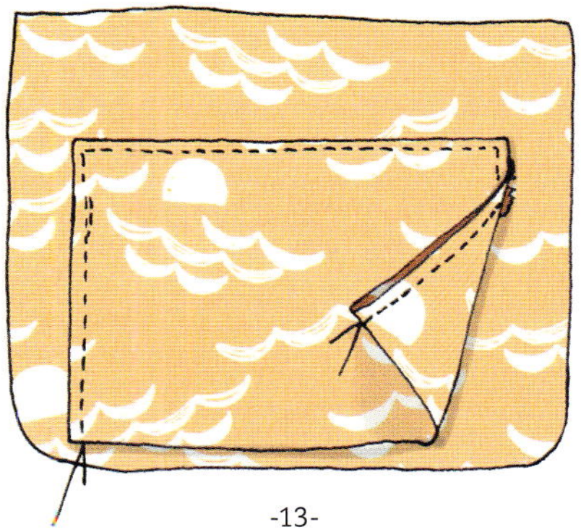

-13-

-14-

-15-

-16-

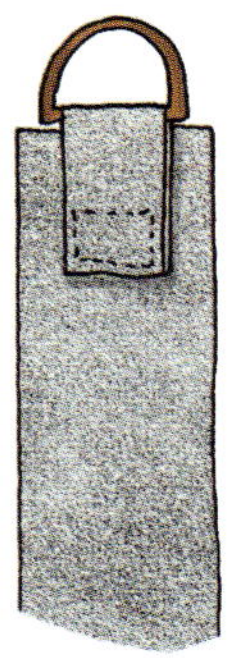

-17-

The Exterior Pocket

- With a knife, cut out the slit in the location shown on the pattern. On each end, glue a piece of reinforcing leather. Once the glue is dry, stitch them in place at ⅛" from the edge (18).

- Iron the interfacing onto the underside of the pocket's lining. Place the pocket on the main part of the bag, right side of the fabric against the underside of the leather, in the location shown on the pattern. Fix the pocket in place with masking tape and then stitch all around the border at 3⁄16" from the edge (19).

Finishing the Bag

- Place the female part of the snap fastener on the leather front piece.

- Assemble the leather strip and the leather front, stitching it at ⅜" from the edge (evenly, as you did with the lining) (see 14).

- Assemble the other side of the strip and the main part of the bag in the same way (see 15).

- Turn the bag right side out, place the flap in position on the back of the bag (in the location shown on the pattern), and stitch it 3⁄16" from the edge (20).

- Slip the lining into the bag, fold the top edges over, and stitch them at ⅛" from the edge (21).

- Attach the chain onto the rings on each side.

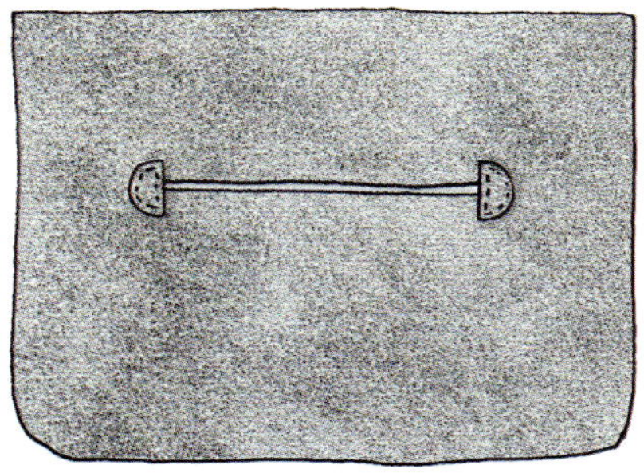

-18-

-19-

-20-

-21-

Pearlescent Shoulder Bag: Pattern

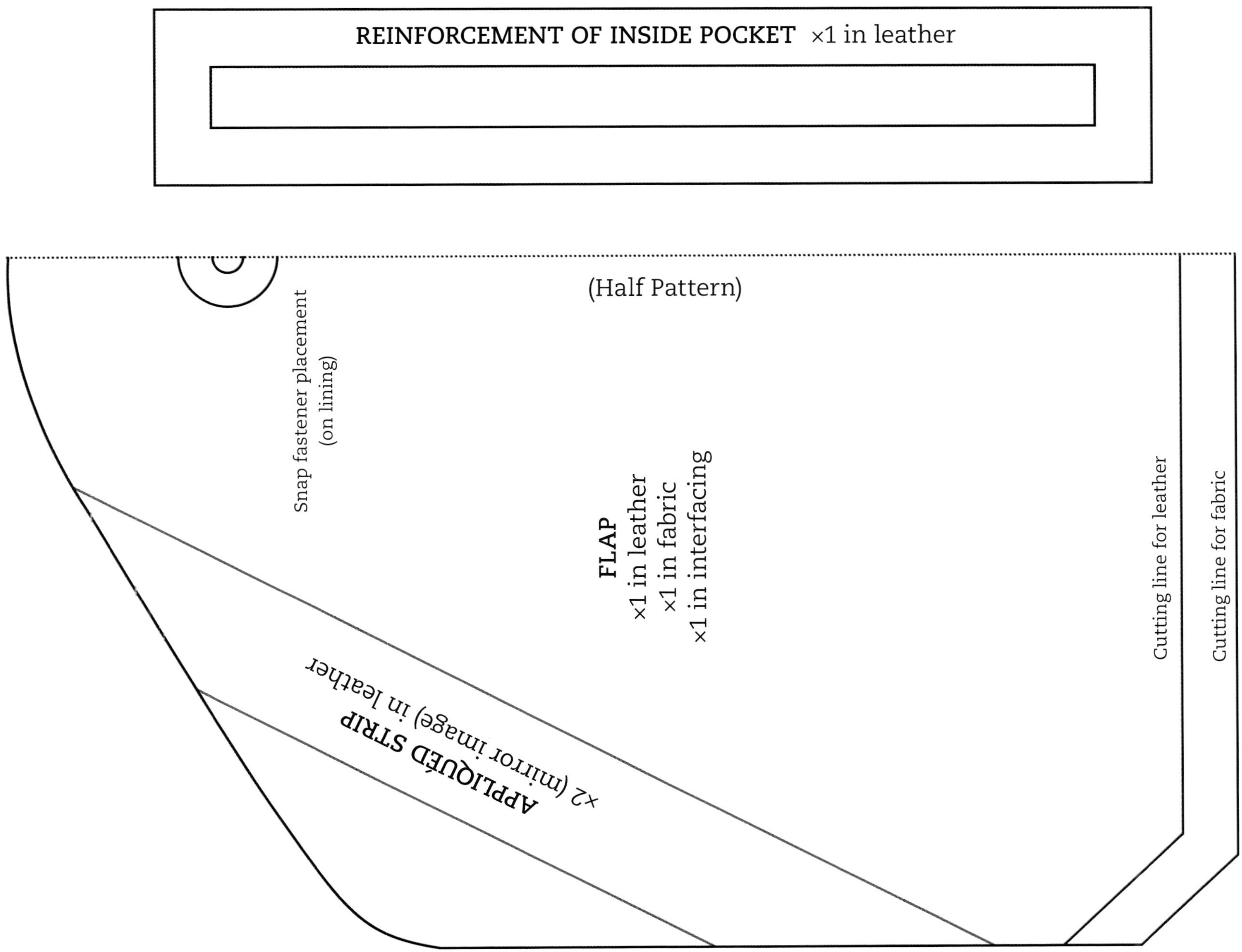

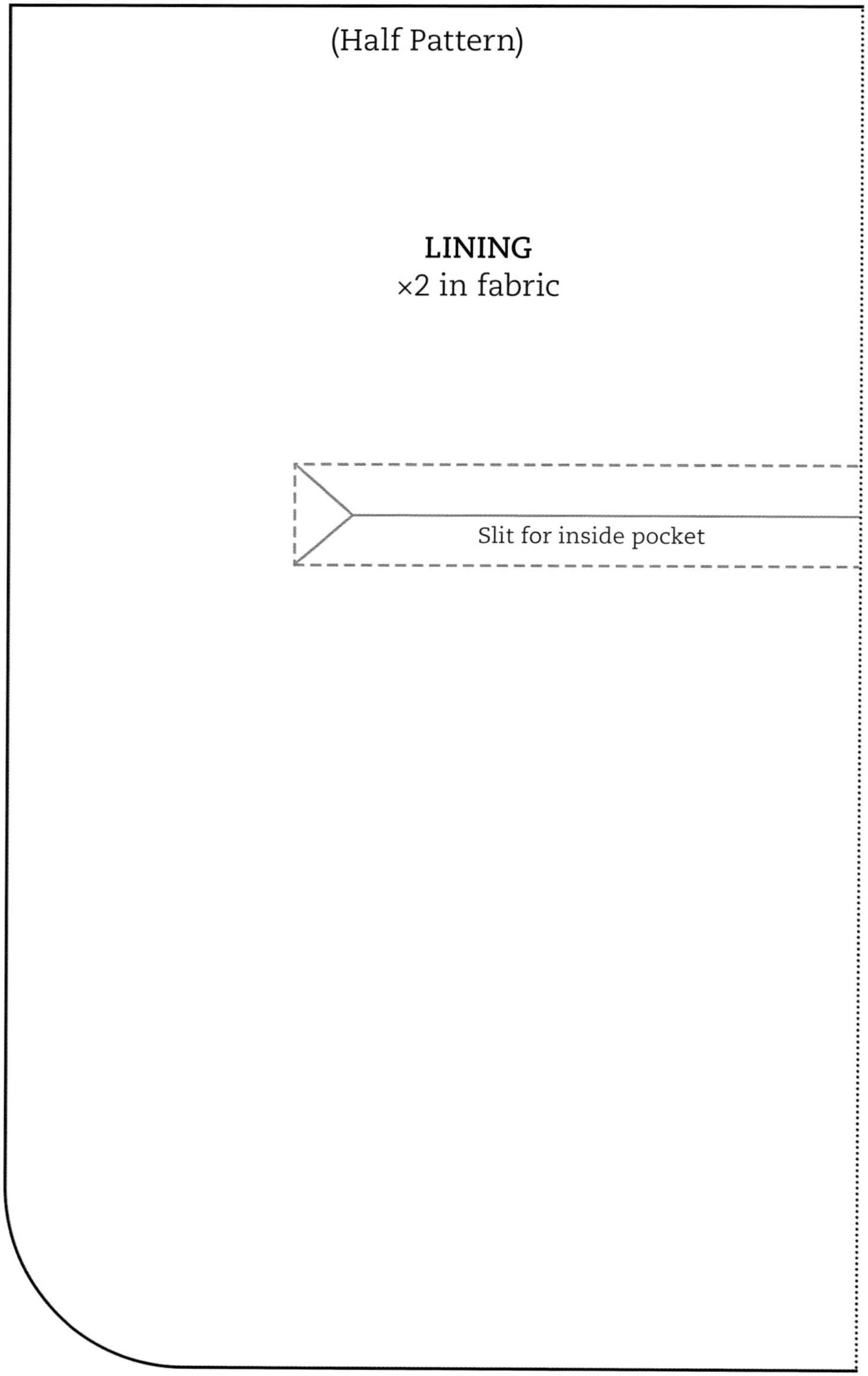
(Half Pattern)
LINING
×2 in fabric
Slit for inside pocket

LINING OF BACK POCKET
×1 in fabric
×1 in interfacing

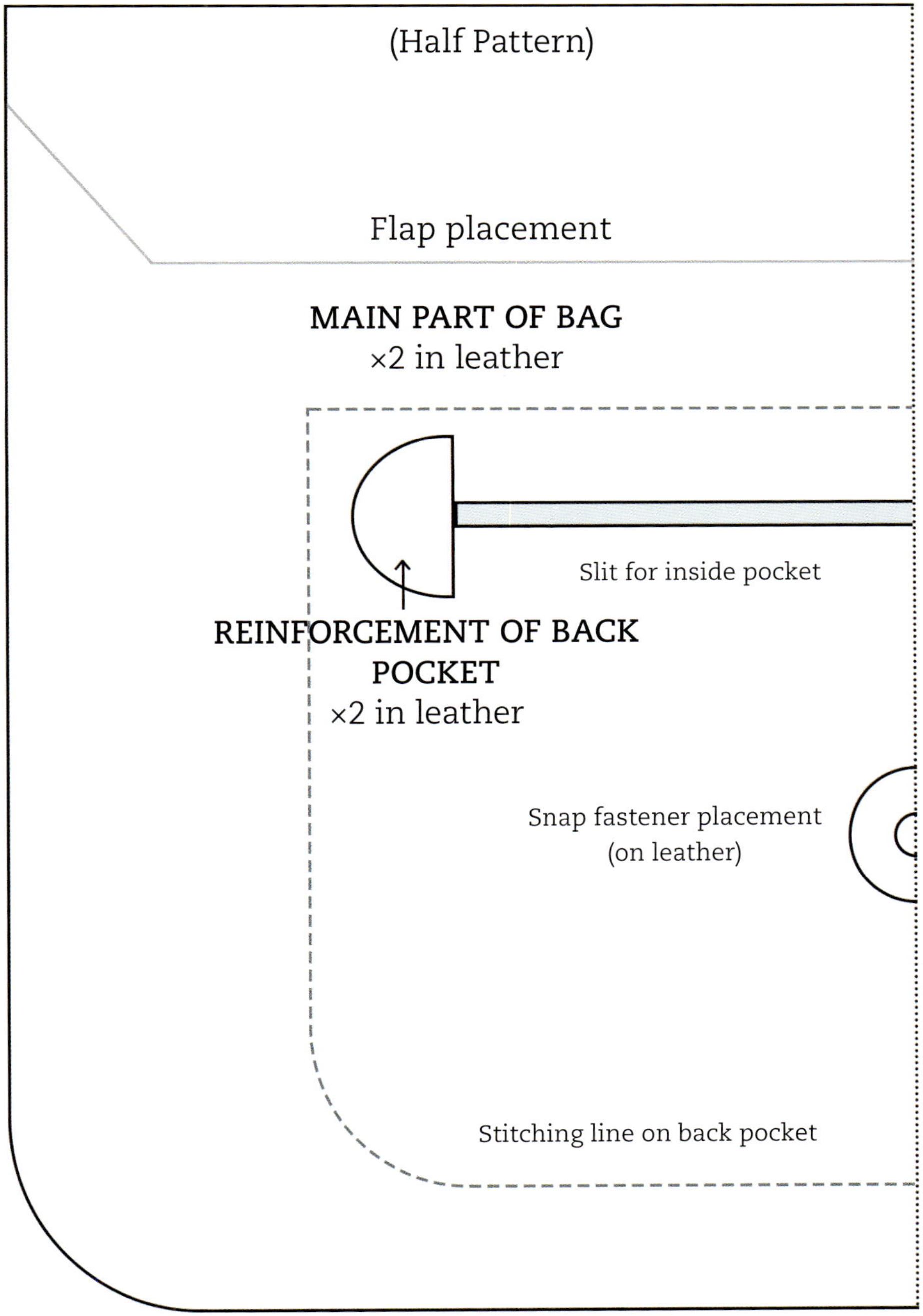
(Half Pattern)
Flap placement
MAIN PART OF BAG
×2 in leather
Slit for inside pocket
REINFORCEMENT OF BACK
POCKET
×2 in leather
Snap fastener placement
(on leather)
Stitching line on back pocket

Navajo-Style Purse and Cuff Bracelet

DIFFICULTY LEVEL: ☆☆
Techniques: straight stitch (machine), inserting a zipper, stencil painting
Materials: leather sewing-machine needle (size 14/90), Teflon presser foot, zipper foot, hot iron, card stock, knife, stencil brush
Recommended leather: thin, supple leather without finishing treatment so that the paint can easily penetrate
Dimensions: 5½" × 8¼"

You'll need:

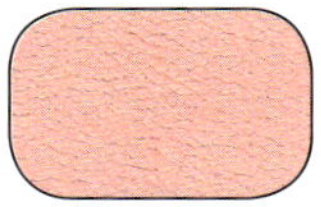 Rose blush lambskin: 9¾" × 13¾"

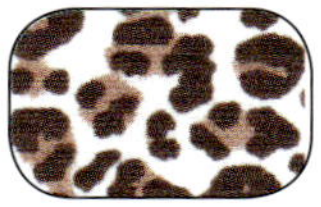 Cotton fabric: 9¾" × 13¾"

1 metal-toothed zipper, 7" long

Leather paints: gold, black, white

Stencil brush, 3⁄16" diameter

1 snap-hook chain, approx. 36" long (optional)

CUTTING

- ***Main part of the purse:*** Cut out two rectangles 9" × 6" of leather.
- ***Lining:*** Cut out two rectangles 9" × 6" of fabric.
- ***Zipper ends:*** Cut out two rectangles 1¼" × 1½" of fabric.
- ***Loops:*** Cut out two bands 3⁄16" × 1¼" of leather.

The purse, very easy to sew, is decorated with a stenciled pattern. The two small loops on each end give you the option to attach a fine chain and use it as a shoulder bag. The cuff is made up of pieces of appliquéd leather. Quick and easy to make, it's an ideal gift!

PURSE INSTRUCTIONS

Painting

- Prepare your stencils: print the three patterns on card stock, then cut the patterns out with a knife.

- Place the white stencil on the center of one of the leather rectangles (there should be a margin of $\frac{3}{8}$" all around the stencil). Hold it in place with one hand and, with the other, dip the brush into the white paint. Dab the brush on another sheet of paper to remove the excess paint and then dab the paint on the openings in the stencil. Use only very small amounts of paint each time—the brush should be almost dry. As soon as you have completed a pattern, lift the stencil slightly from the leather (the paint dries very fast and the stencil might stick to the leather). Once you have finished all the patterns, leave the paint to dry for about an hour and then stencil on a second coat of white paint (1).

- Proceed in the same way for the gold stencil (2) and then the black (3), leaving the paint to dry thoroughly between colors. For these two colors a single coat is sufficient.

-1-

-2-

-3-

Inserting the Zipper

- Iron a $\frac{3}{16}$" fold on each end of the two fabric rectangles and fold them in two (4).

- Cut the zipper to leave $\frac{1}{2}$" at each end (5), then slip the two small pieces of fabric onto each end and stitch them across $\frac{1}{8}$" from the edge (6).

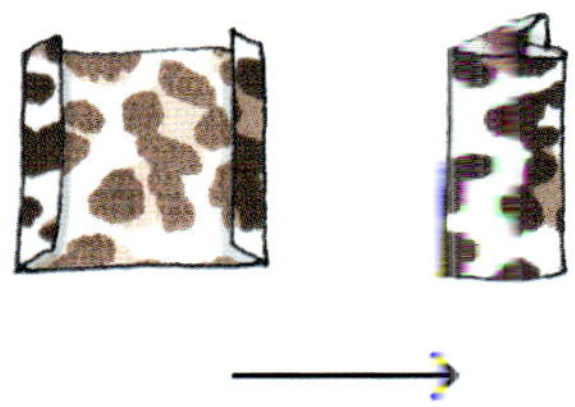

-4-

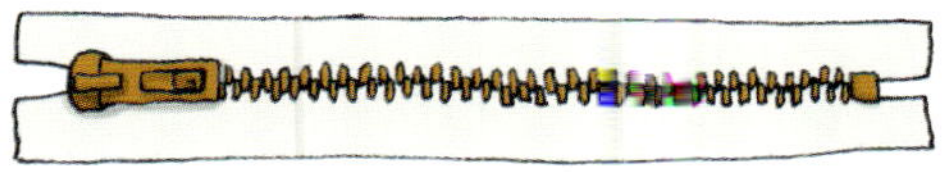

-5-

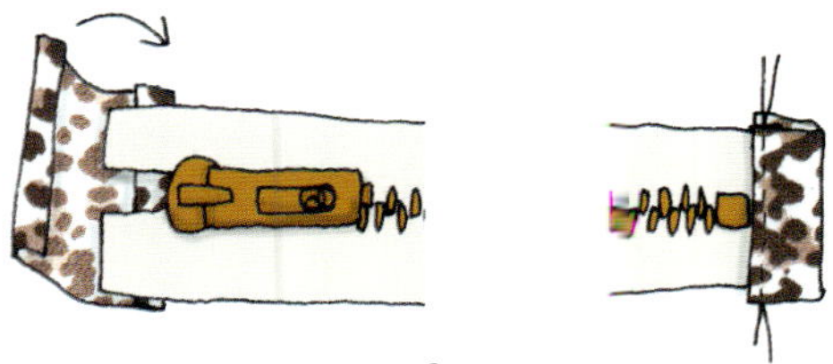

-6-

- Place the zipper on the edge of one of the leather rectangles, right sides together, leaving ½" of leather free at each end. Place one of the lining pieces on top, the wrong side facing you. Fix the pieces together with paper clips. Install the zipper foot onto your machine and stitch the pieces ¼" from the edge (7).

- Proceed in the same manner for the other part of the zipper.

- With the Teflon presser foot in place, edgestitch ⅛" from the edge along the seams of the zipper, on the leather side (8).

Finishing the Purse

- Fold the two small strips of leather in two to create the small loops and stitch them onto the leather at 1⁄16" from the edge (9).

- Open the zipper halfway and position the piece so that the two leather parts are against each other. To keep everything in place, pin the lining and use paper clips on the leather. Stitch all around at ⅜" from the edge, leaving an opening of 4" in the lining (10).

- Clip the corners.

- Turn the purse right side out through the opening and then close with blind stitch.

- Slip the lining into the purse.

-9-

-7-

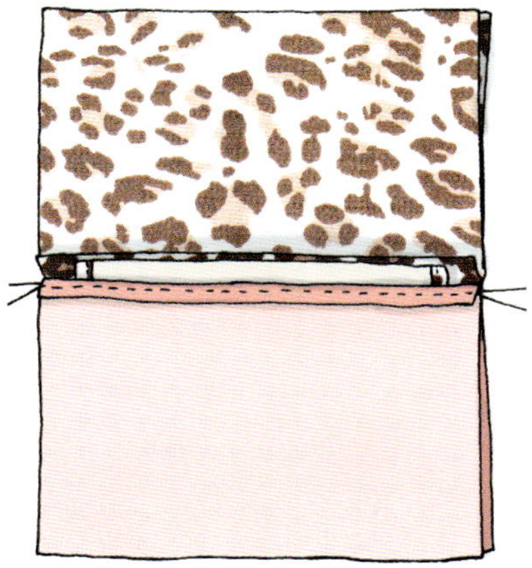

-8-

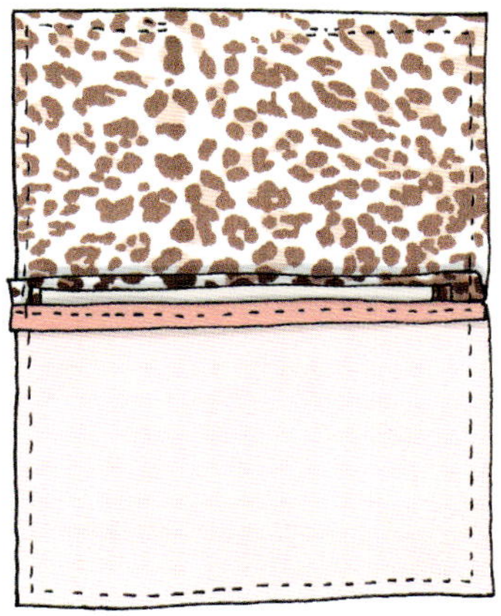

-10-

WHITE STENCIL

GOLD STENCIL

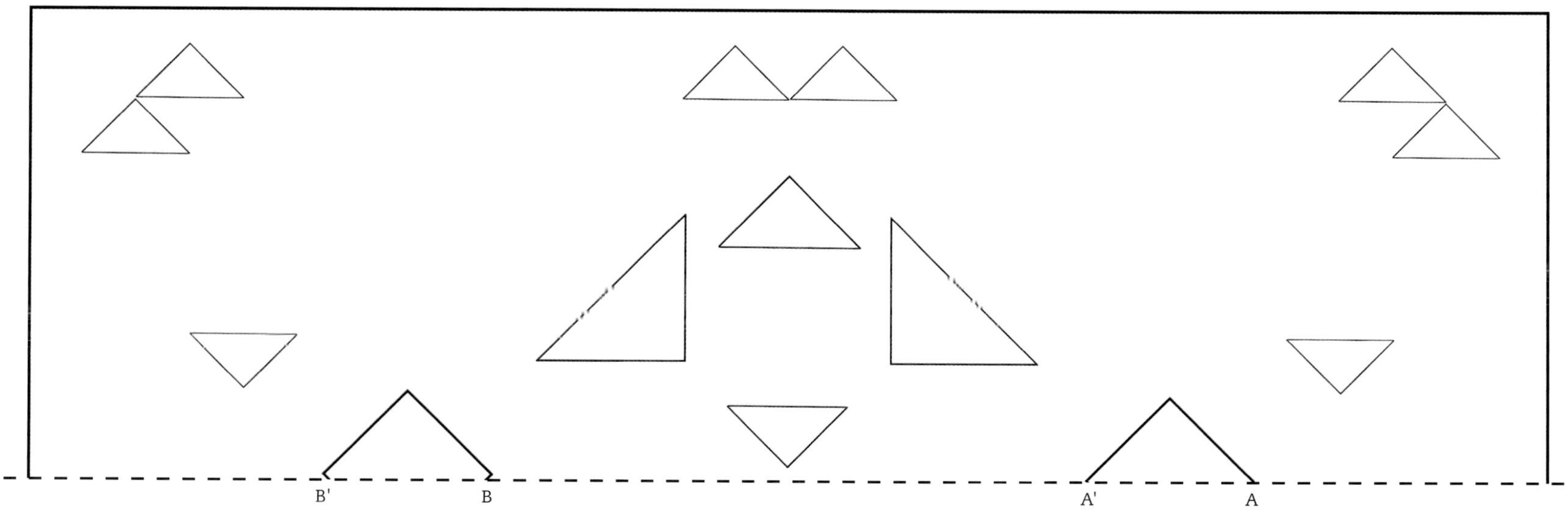

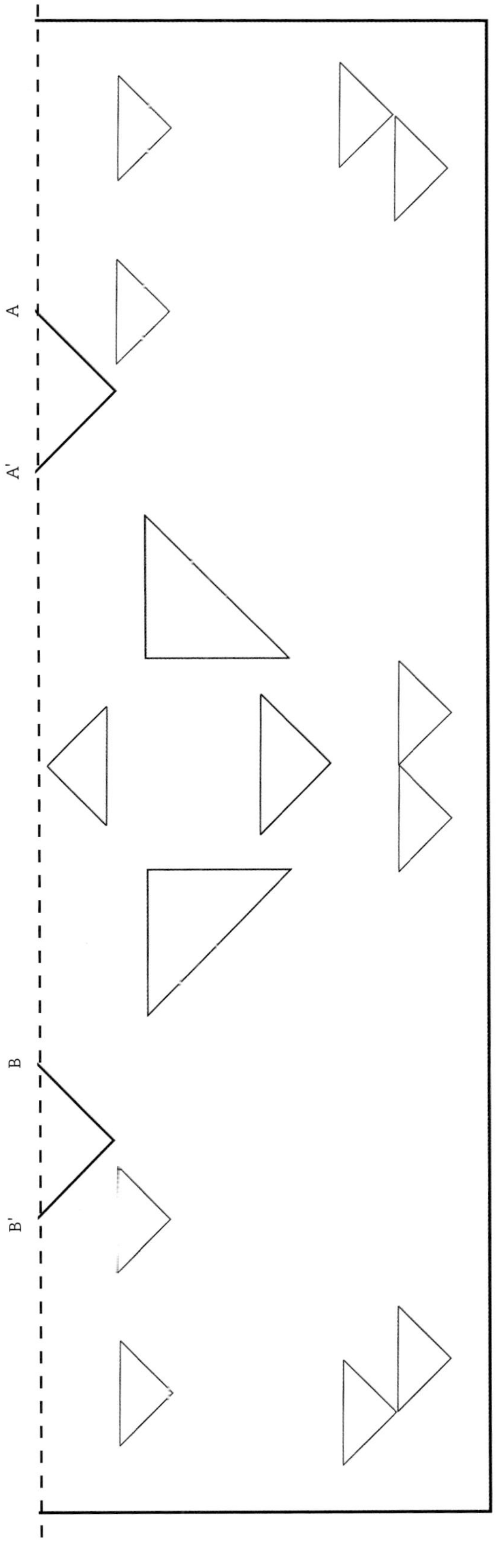

BLACK STENCIL

Navajo Cuff Bracelet

DIFFICULTY LEVEL: ☆
Techniques: straight stitch (machine), collage, setting studs
Materials: leather sewing-machine needle (size 14/90), Teflon presser foot, punch pliers, leather glue, brush, knife
Recommended leather: For the bracelet, thick leather. For the appliqués, thin leather.
Dimensions: 1½" × 7½"

You'll need:

Black spangled suede calfskin: 1½" × 7½"

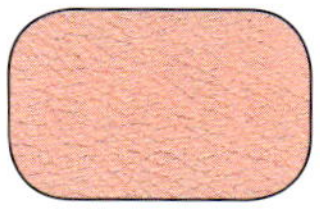

Rose blush lambskin: a small scrap

Gold goatskin: a small scrap

2 studs, 3/16" diameter

INSTRUCTIONS

- Start by sticking small gold leather triangles on the larger pink leather triangles (1).
- Then glue the different appliqués on the black leather band, following the pattern (2).
- Once the glue is dry, edge stitch each of the appliqués at ⅛" from the edge (3).
- With the punch pliers (⅛" diameter), make two holes in the locations marked on the pattern and then cut two 3/16" slits (on the opposite end) for the studs (4).
- Screw the studs onto the other end (5).

CUTTING

- *Base of the cuff:* Cut a band out of the black leather.
- *Appliqués:* Cut out the shapes shown on the pattern.

-1-

-2-

-3-

-4-

-5-

Cuff Bracelet: Pattern

— Cut from gold leather

— Cut from pink leather

Envelope-Style Purse and Smartphone Case

Difficulty level: ☆
Techniques: straight stitch (machine); setting rivets, eyelets, and studs
Materials: leather sewing-machine needle (size 16/100), Teflon presser foot, mallet, leather-marking pen, knife, punch pliers, tools for setting rivets and eyelets (supplied with the rivets and eyelets), leather glue, screwdriver
Recommended leather: For the purse: fairly stiff, thick leather. For the inset: thinner leather.
Dimensions: 9½" × 5¾" (purse closed)

You'll need:

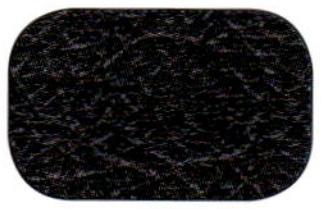

Black natural-grain goatskin, 5 oz. / 2 mm thick: 21¾" × 17¾"

Striped calfskin, 2 oz. / 1 mm thick: 7⅞" × 9¾"

2 tubular rivets, 3⁄16" to ¼" thick

2 eyelets, 9⁄16" diameter

1 stud, 3⁄16" diameter

55" silver chain

Amazing as it might seem, this purse is put together without sewing! It's made up of a single piece of leather, folded and held in place by rivets; a minimum of effort for maximum effect.

The smartphone case has a secret pocket in which you can slip your credit card or some cash.

CUTTING

- *Main part of the purse:* Copy the pattern onto a 21¾" × 17¾" sheet of paper (see the diagram below of the full pattern) and then cut it out of the black leather, marking the different locations with the leather-marking pen.
- *Inset:* Trace the pattern for the inset and cut it out of the striped leather.
- *Slide for the shoulder strap:* Cut the strip once out of the black leather and once out of the striped leather.

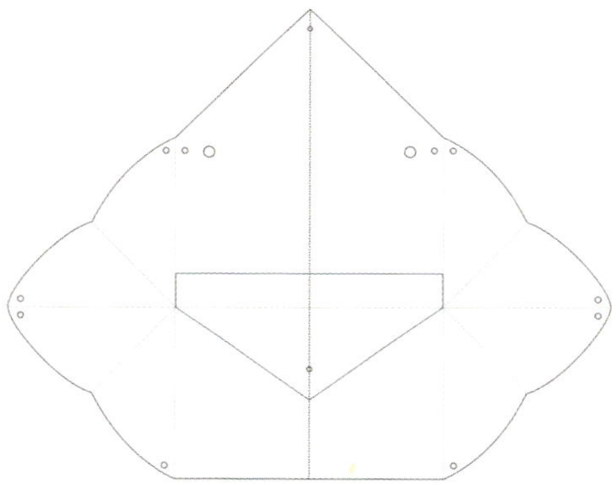

The full pattern

PURSE INSTRUCTIONS

Making the Purse

- Locate where the inset is to be placed on the main part of the purse, and glue it on with the leather glue (1).
- Install the leather needle and Teflon presser foot onto your machine.
- Once the glue is dry, do a decorative edgestitch all around the inset at ⅛" from the edge with a stitch length of ⅛".
- Make the holes in the places where the eyelets will go (usually the little tool to make the holes is supplied with the eyelets) and then set them, following the instructions on the packet (2).
- With the punch pliers (⅛" tip), make a hole for the stud in the spot indicated on the inset.
- Insert the stud in the hole and screw it on the right side of the leather (3).
- In the spot for the stud slit on the flap (see pattern), make a small 3⁄16" hole with the punch pliers and a small ⅛" slit with a knife to enlarge the hole (4).
- Using the small tool supplied with the rivets, make the holes in the locations indicated on the pattern—holes 1 to 5 (5).

-3-

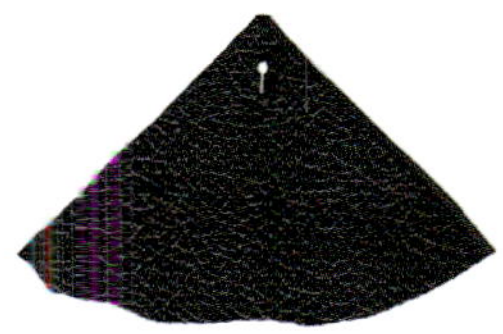

-4-

-1-

-2-

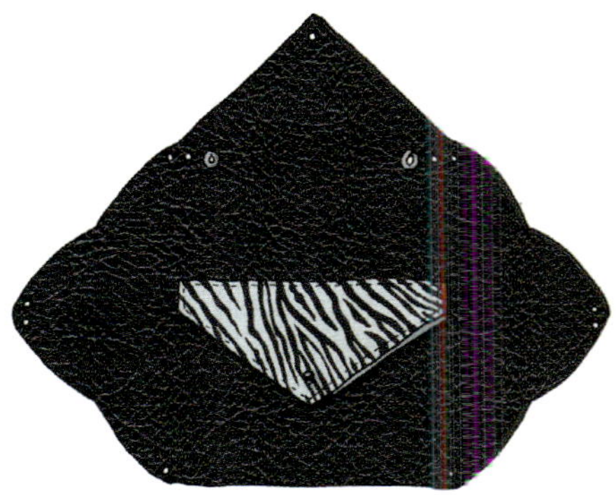

-5-

- Fold the leather as shown in the drawings, along the gray dotted lines shown on the pattern, making sure that the rivet holes match up (6 & 7). At each fold, press down on the folds to mark them or tap them with the rounded head of a mallet.

- Insert the male part of a rivet into hole #5 (on the inside of the purse) and bring it out through hole #1 (on the outside of the purse). Set the female part of the rivet and then attach the two parts together with the mallet and the little tool supplied with the rivets (8). Do the same for the other rivet.

Making the Slide

- Cut slits into the black leather strip with a knife.

- Place the two parts wrong sides together and stitch all around at ⅛" from the edge with a stitch length of ⅛" (9).

- Slip the chain through the slits in the slide (10). Thread the chain through the two eyelets and then join the two links at each end to close the chain.

-8-

-9-

-10-

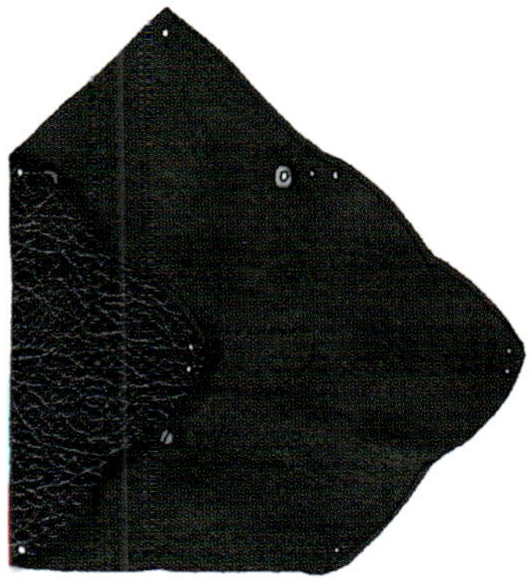

-6-

-7-

Envelope-Style Purse: Half Pattern

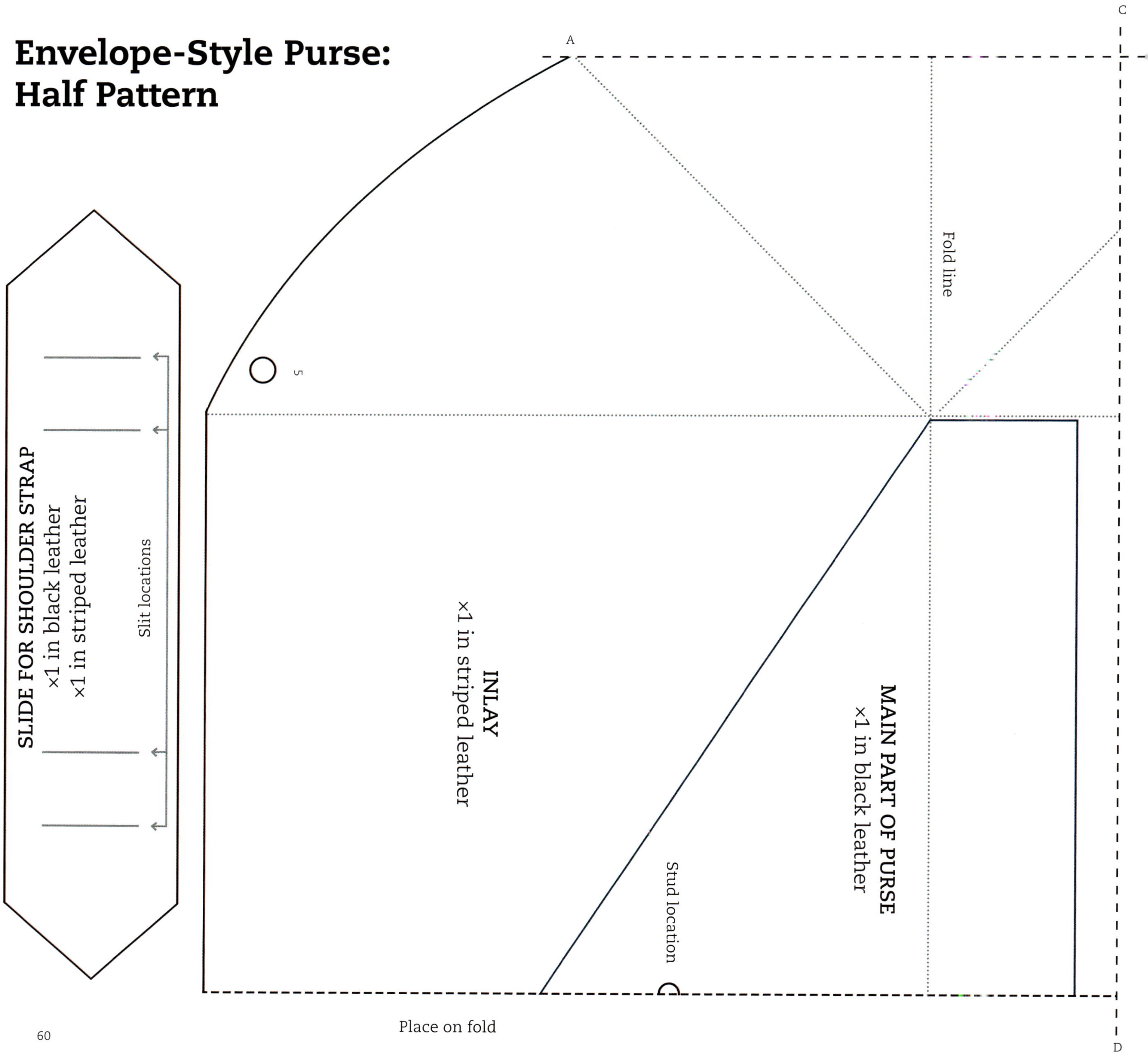

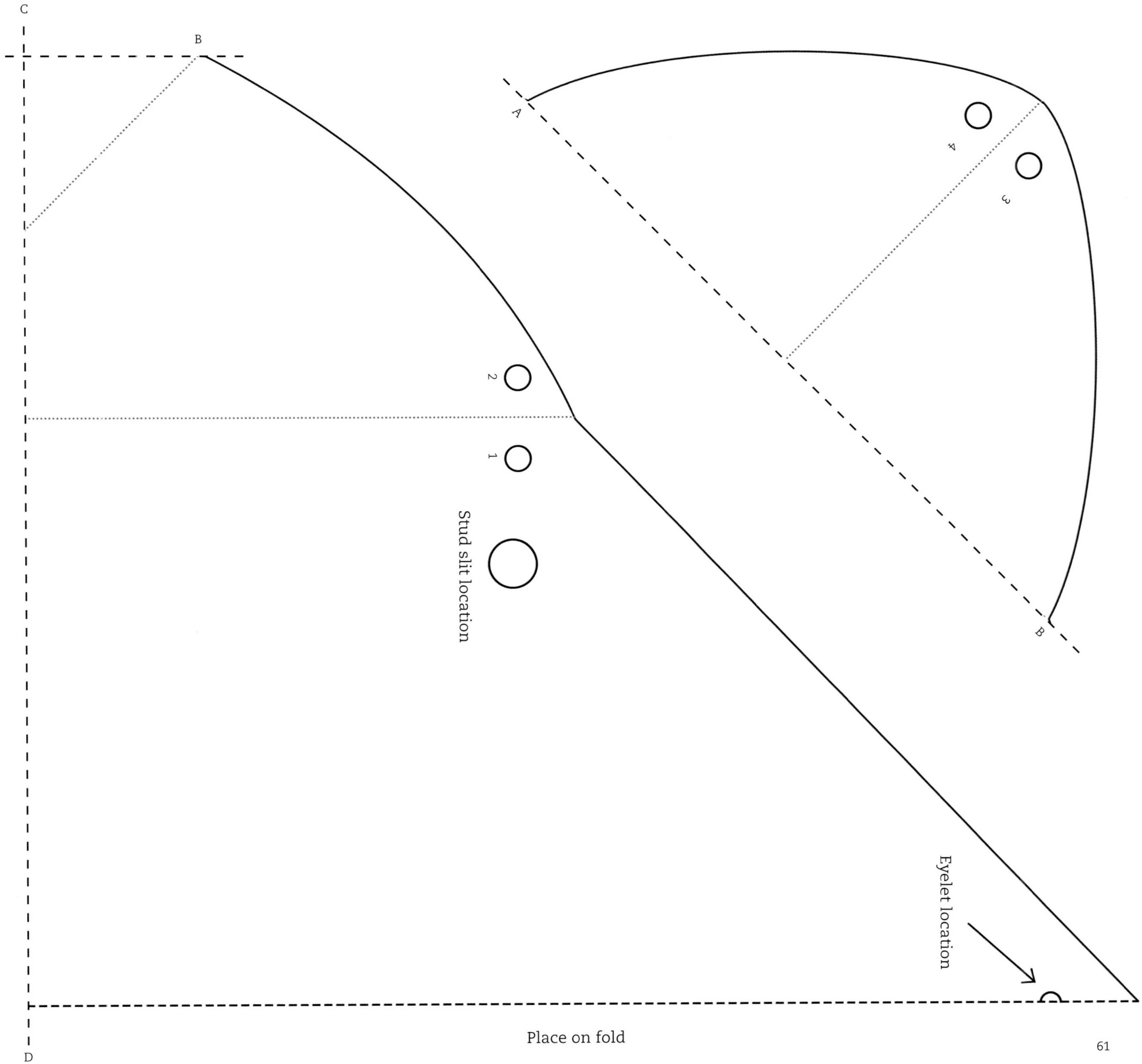
C
B
A
4
3
B
2
1
Stud slit location
Eyelet location
Place on fold
D

Smartphone Case

Difficulty level: ☆
Techniques: straight stitch (machine)
Materials: leather sewing-machine needle (size 16/100), Teflon presser foot
Recommended leather: Fairly thick, stiff leather such as natural-grain goatskin or suede. Be careful: in some places you'll be stitching three layers of leather at the same time, so do a test with scraps to make sure your machine is up to stitching the leathers you have chosen.
Dimensions: 5" × 3⅛" for size 1 (for a telephone 2⅜" wide, 4¾" high, and ⅜" thick maximum) and 5⅛" × 4" for size 2 (for a telephone 2⅜" wide, 5" high, and 5/16" thick)

You'll need:

Striped suede calfskin: 6" × 11¾"

Black and silver elastic:

7" long for size 1

6¾" long for size 2

CUTTING

- *Main part of the case:* Cut the pattern twice out of the leather.

- *Front pocket:* Cut the pattern once out of the leather.

INSTRUCTIONS

- Install a leather needle and Teflon presser foot onto your machine. Set a straight-stitch length of ⅛". On each of the three pieces of leather, do a decorative straight stitch 1/16" from the edge: on the upper edge for the two main parts; on the upper edge and the right side (from point A to point B) on the front pocket (1).

- Fold the elastic band in two, right sides together. Place it on the location marked on the pattern on one of the main parts of the case (placing the end of the band ⅜" in from the edge), and fix it in place with masking tape (2).

- Place the second main part of the case over the first, wrong sides together, then stitch around the three sides at ⅛" from the edge, doing a backstitch at the start and at the end (3).

- Place the pocket on the front of the case and stitch the left side and bottom side (from point B to point A) at ⅛" from the edge (4).

- Fold the elastic band around the case to keep it in place (see the photo on the next page).

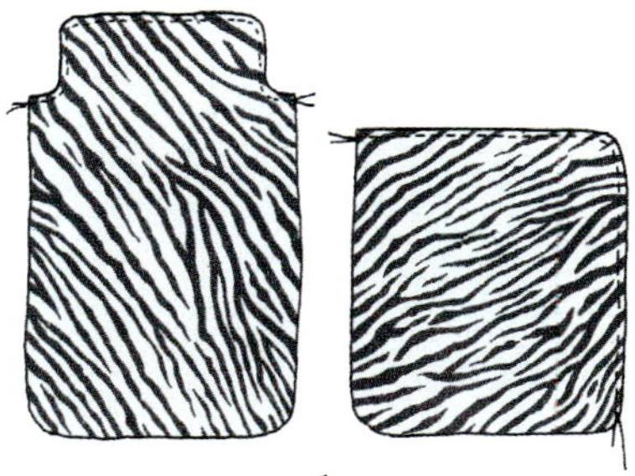

-1-

-3-

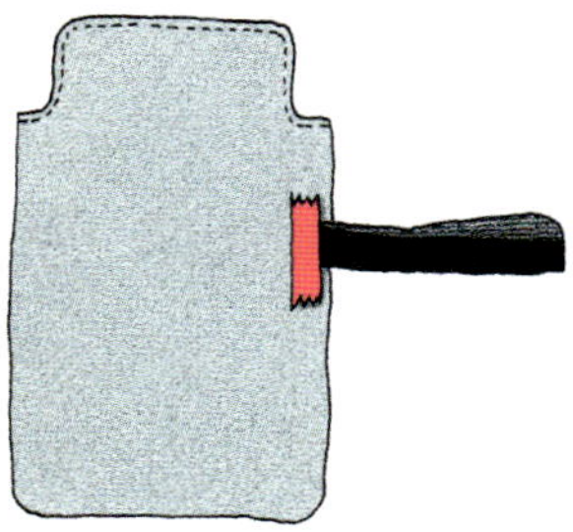

-2-

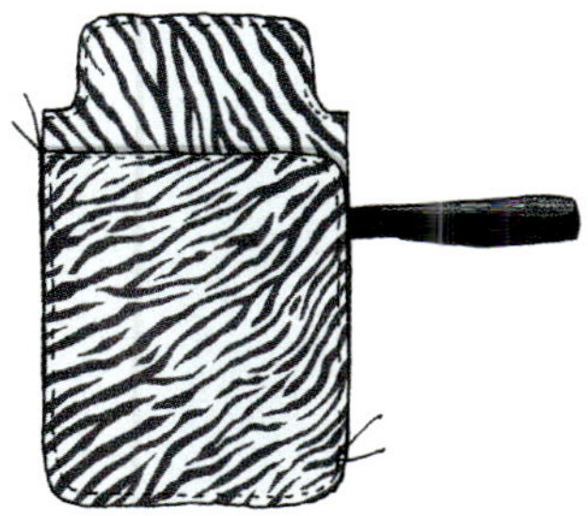

-4-

Smartphone Case: Pattern

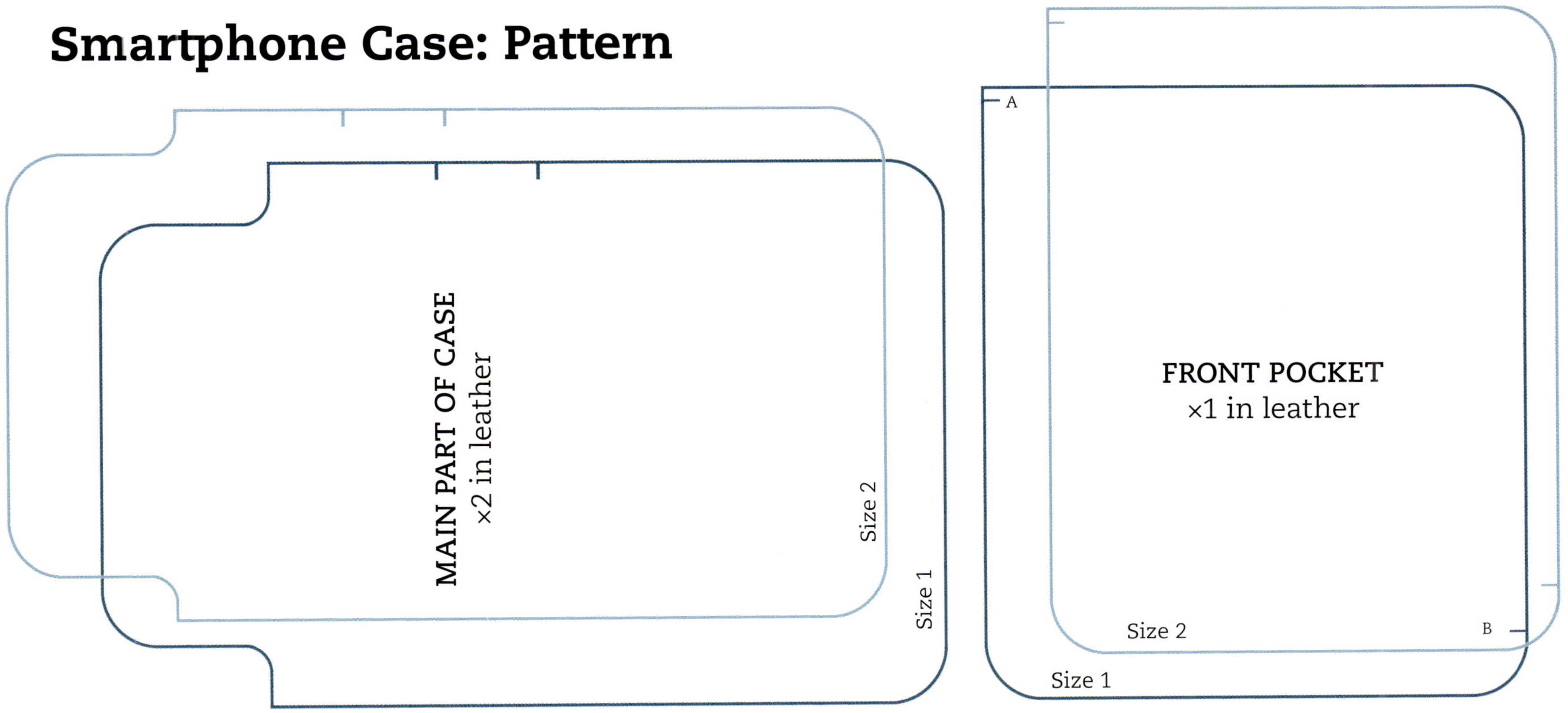

Baby Moccasins

DIFFICULTY LEVEL: ☆☆
Materials: leather sewing-machine needle, Teflon presser foot, safety pin
Recommended leather: thin, supple leather such as lambskin or suede goatskin (vegetable tanned, to avoid risking allergies in small children)
Dimensions: 3 months (foot length 3⅛"), 6 months (foot length 4¼"), and 12 months (foot length 5⅛").

You'll need:

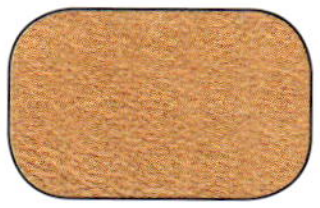

Mustard-yellow lambskin: 11¾" × 15¾"

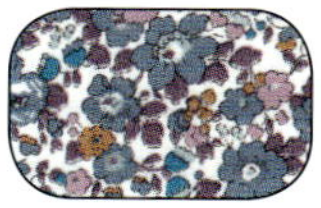

Cotton fabric (for the lining): 11¾" × 15¾"

Cord or other trim, for ties: two pieces 19¾" long each

Elastic, 3/16" wide, two pieces: 6" (3 months), 6¾" (6 months), or 7½" (12 months)

CUTTING

- *Sole:* Cut twice (mirror image) out of the leather and twice out of the lining. Mark the locations indicated on the pattern with a leather-marking pen.
- *Top of the foot:* Cut twice (mirror image) out of the leather and twice out of the lining. Mark the locations indicated on the pattern and cut the slits with a knife (only in the leather).
- *Back of the foot:* Cut twice out of the leather. Mark the locations indicated on the pattern.
- *Fringed band:* Cut twice out of the leather. Mark the locations indicated on the pattern.

We love these trendy, comfortable little shoes that won't fall off your little one's feet thanks to the little elastic band just above the ankles. Maybe these moccasins will accompany his or her first steps?

INSTRUCTIONS (FOR MAKING ONE SHOE)

Making the Top of the Shoe

- Place the fabric pieces of the two top parts of the shoe against each other, right sides together, and stitch the central seam 3/16" from the edge (1).

- Open the seam with a hot iron to flatten it out.

- Install the leather needle and Teflon presser foot onto your machine. Place the leather pieces of the two top parts of the shoe against each other, right sides together, and hold them in place with paper clips. Stitch the central seam at 3/16" from the edge (the same as for the fabric).

- Open the seam to flatten it and stitch each side 1/8" from the center to keep the folds flat (2).

- Place the two top parts of the shoe (leather and fabric), right sides together, matching up the central seams. Hold them in place with paper clips and stitch the tongue at 1/4" from the edge (3).

- Clip the curved edges and turn it right side out. Topstitch all around the piece at 1/8" from the edge (4).

Making the Back of the Shoe

- Use scissors to make the fringed band; to do this, draw a guide line on the back of the leather band and then cut strips up to the line at 3/16" intervals (5).

- Place the fringed band on the top of the rectangle for the back of the foot (both of the pieces right side up), leaving 3/8" at each end. Stitch at 3/16" from the edge to keep them together (6).

- Place the fabric rectangle over the leather one, right sides together. Hold the pieces in place with paper clips and stitch along the three sides 3/16" from the edge, stopping at the slits to form slide-through areas (don't forget to backstitch each time) (7).

- Clip the corners and turn it right side out.

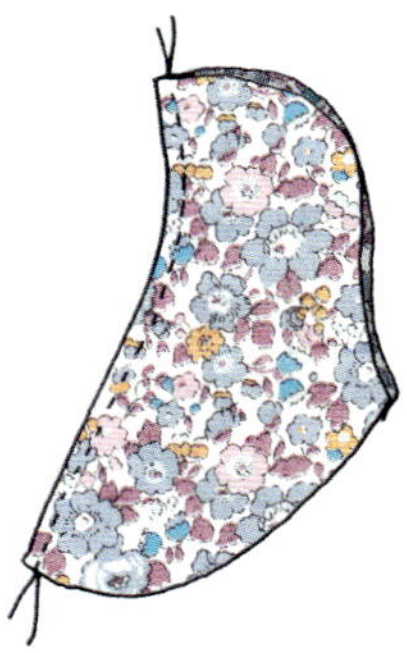

-1-

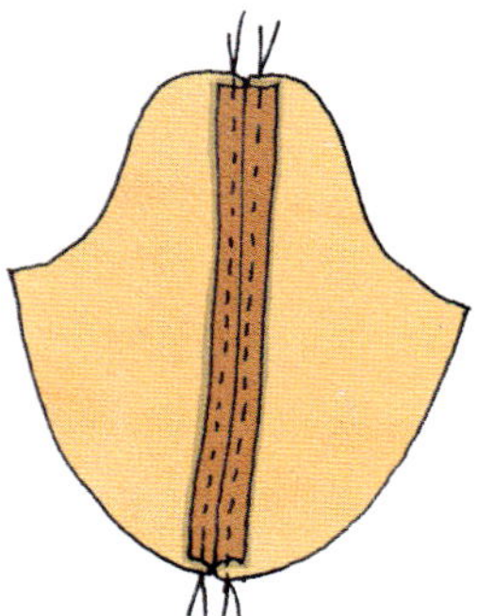

-2-

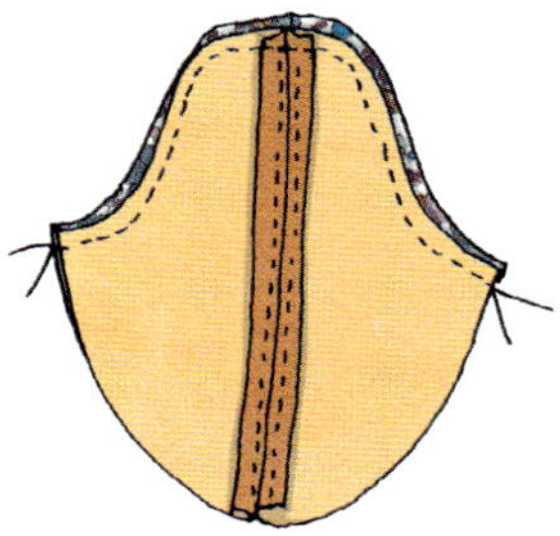

-3-

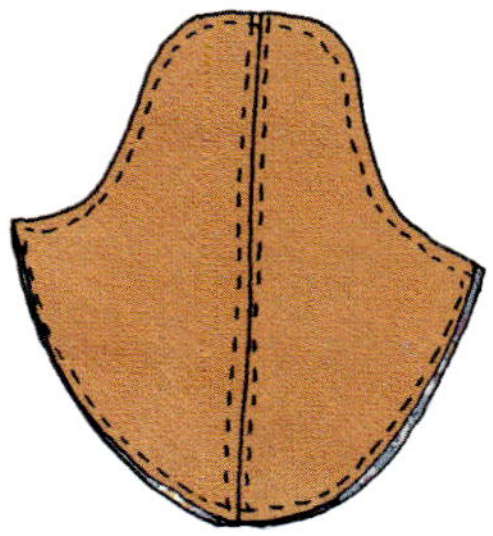

-4-

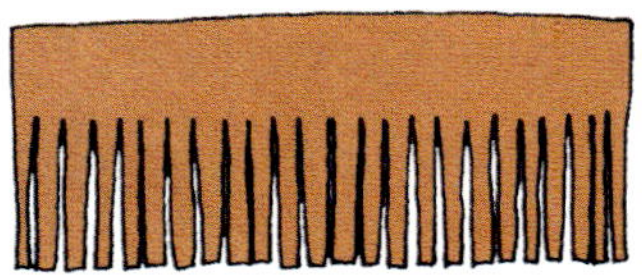

-5-

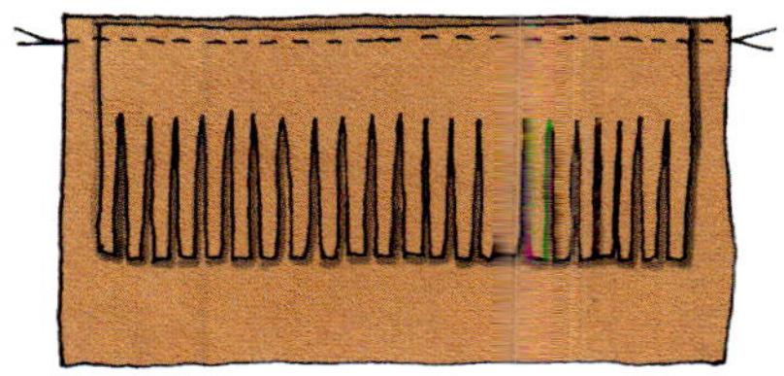

-6-

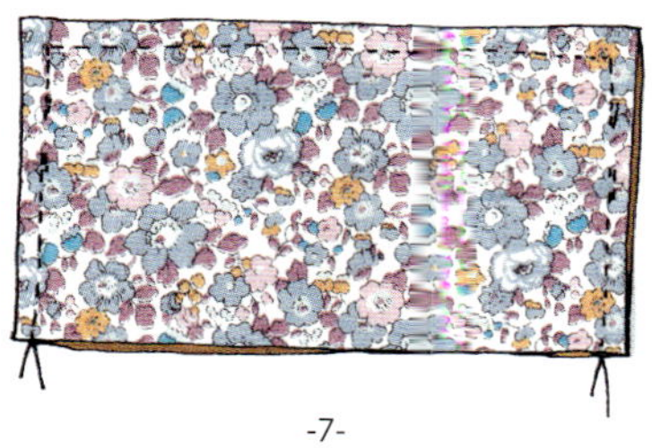

-7-

- Fold back the fringed band and sew two rows of stitches at ¾" and ¼" from the edge (they should correspond to the slits you left earlier) (8).
- Fold the fringed band in place and stitch the three layers at 9⁄16" from the edge (9).

Finishing the Shoe

- Place the fabric sole and the leather sole wrong sides together and stitch them together at 3⁄16" from the edge.
- Place the back band on the sole, leather against leather, matching up the marks A and the heel. Hold it in place with paper clips and stitch 3⁄16" from the edge (10).
- Do the same with the top part of the shoe, matching up the marks B and the center front (11).
- Sew a zigzag stitch around the sole to make it neater.
- Turn the shoe right side out, thread the elastic through the channel by using a safety pin, then pass it through the slits on the top of the shoe and stitch the two ends together (12).
- Thread the cord through the hem of the fringed band, using a safety pin.

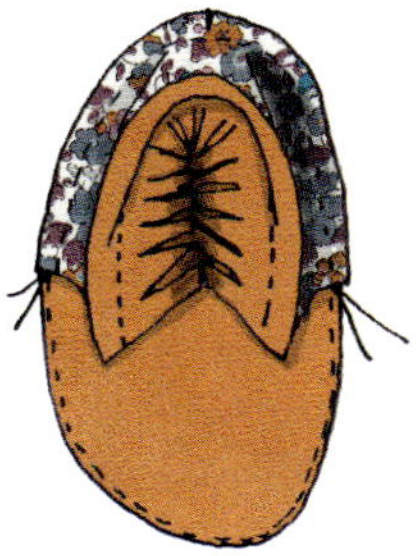
-10-

-11-

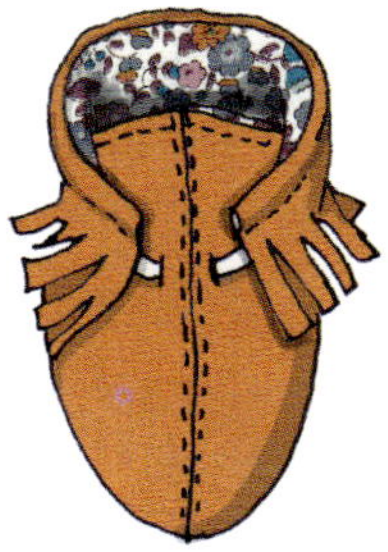
-12-

-8-

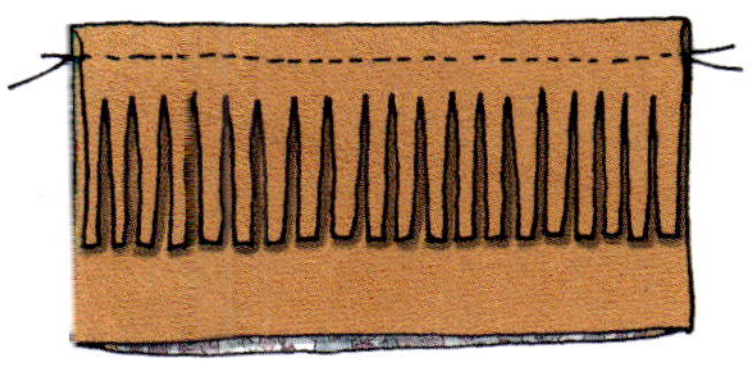
-9-

Baby Moccasins: Pattern

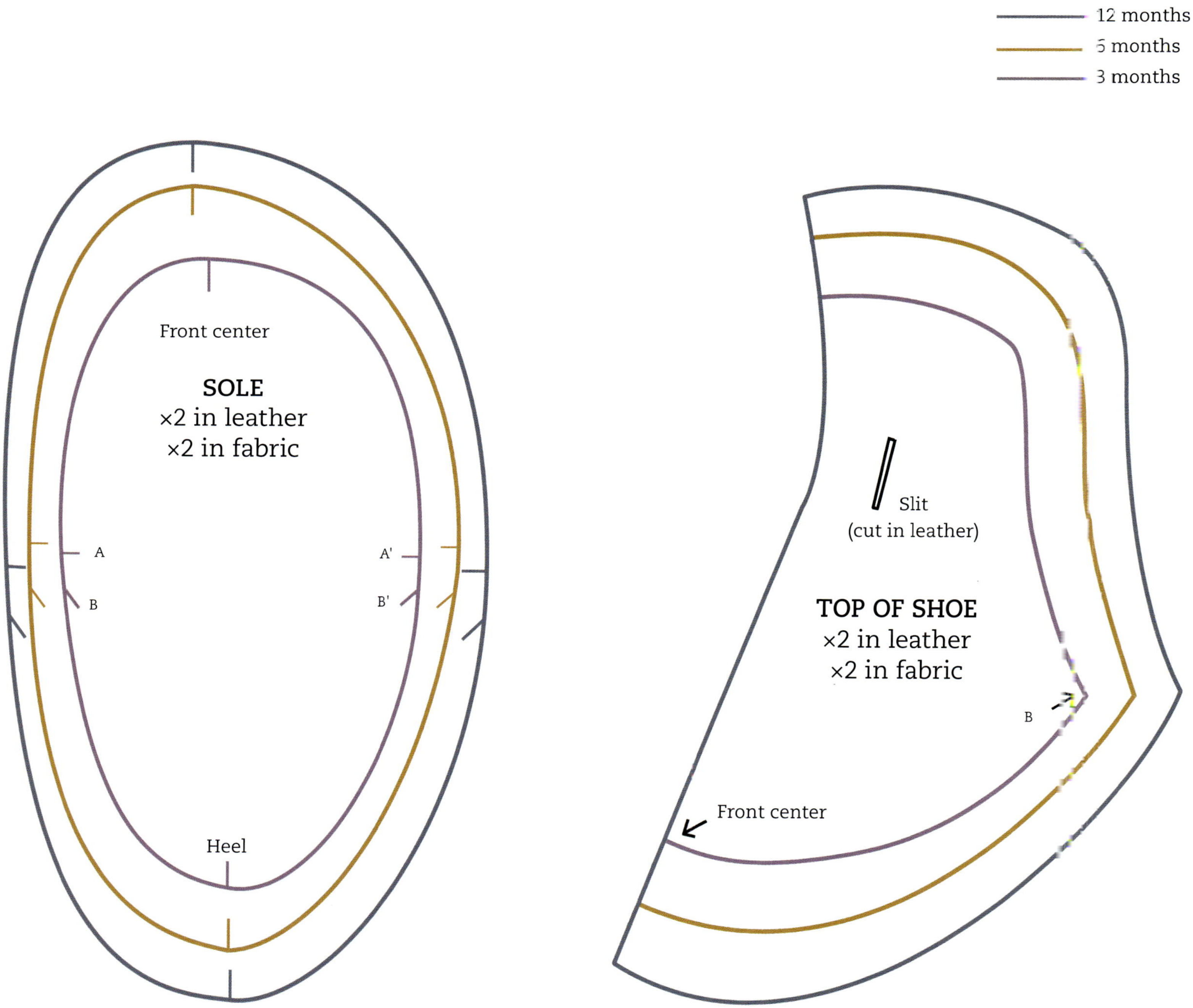

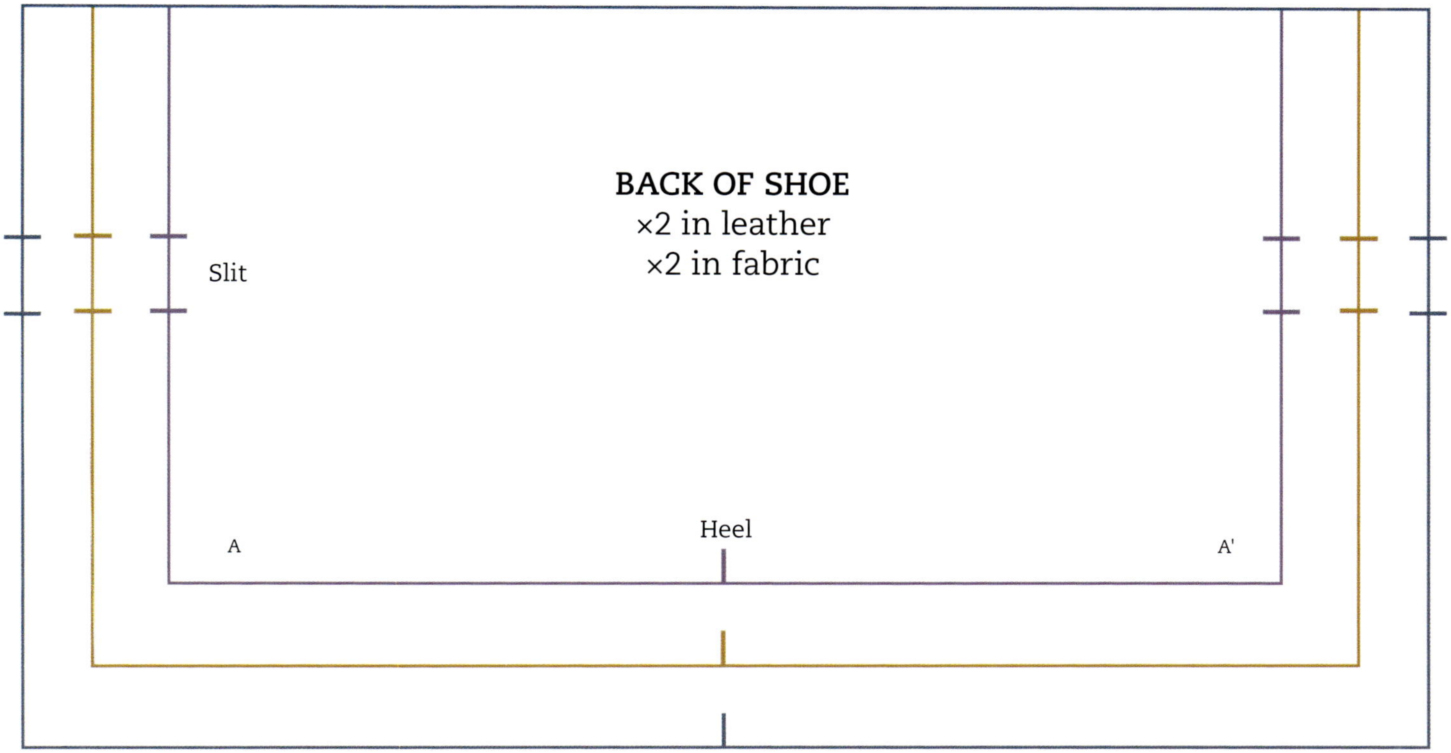
BACK OF SHOE
×2 in leather
×2 in fabric
Slit
A
Heel
A'

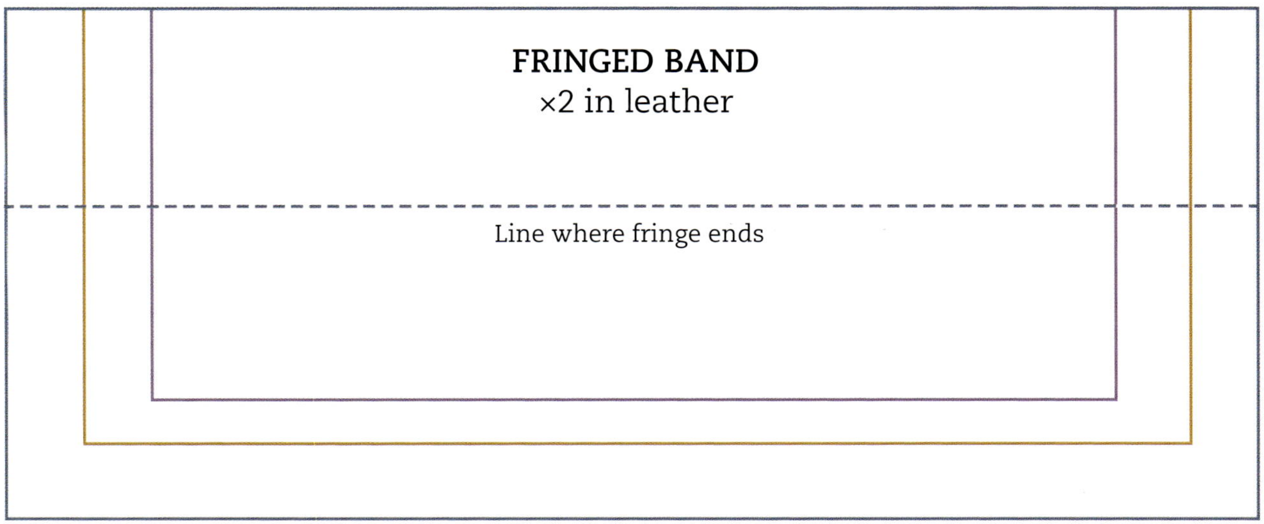
FRINGED BAND
×2 in leather
Line where fringe ends

Cat Shoulder Bag and Fox Change Purse

DIFFICULTY LEVEL: ☆☆
Materials: leather sewing-machine needle, Teflon presser foot, leather glue, knife
Recommended leather: supple leather, but not too thin
Dimensions of the shoulder bag: 7½" × 6" × 1¼"

You'll need:

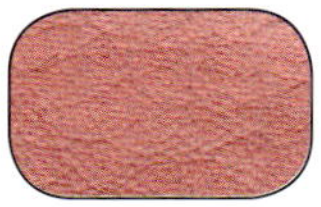

Rose blush pebbled lambskin: 19¾" × 11¾"

Anthracite lambskin: 6" × 4"

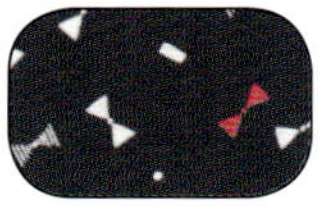

Cotton fabric (for the lining): 20½" × 11¾"

1 packet of mini iron-on cat motifs

1 magnetic snap fastener, 11⁄16" diameter

2 D-rings, 1¼" wide

1 D-ring, 9⁄16" wide

36" strap, 1¼" wide

An adorable set for girls—and not only little girls! The little sparkling cats (yes, you can iron them onto leather!) give the bag lots of charm, and the fox change purse will delight everyone . . .

CUTTING OUT THE BAG

- ***Main part of the bag:*** Cut once out of the pink leather and once out of the fabric.
- ***Front:*** Cut once out of the pink and once out of the fabric.
- ***Strip:*** Cut once out of the pink leather and once out of the fabric.
- ***Loops for the strap:*** Cut two rectangles 3⅛" × 1 1/16" out of the gray leather.
- ***Loop for the tassel:*** Cut a band 2⅜" × ⅜" out of the gray leather.
- ***Tassel:*** Cut the tassel pattern and a band 2⅜" × ¼" out of the gray leather.

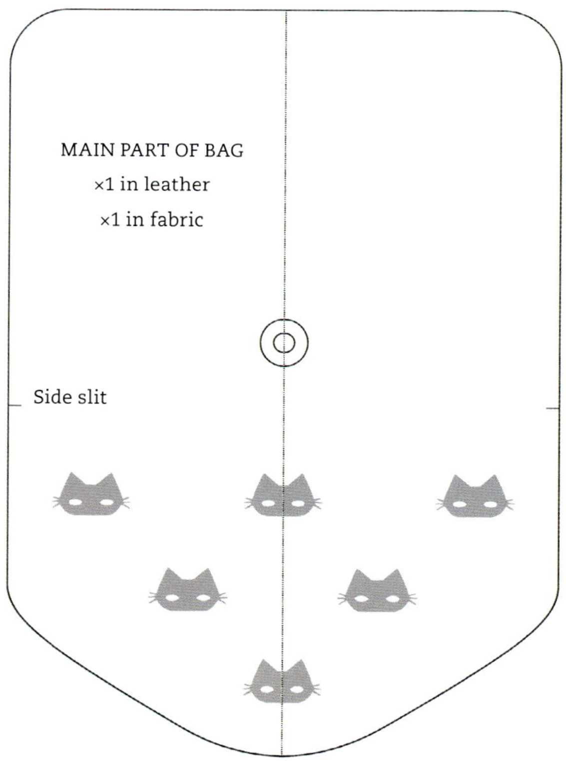

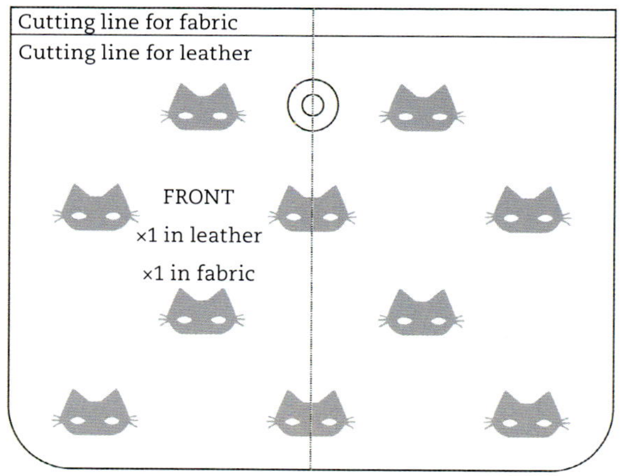

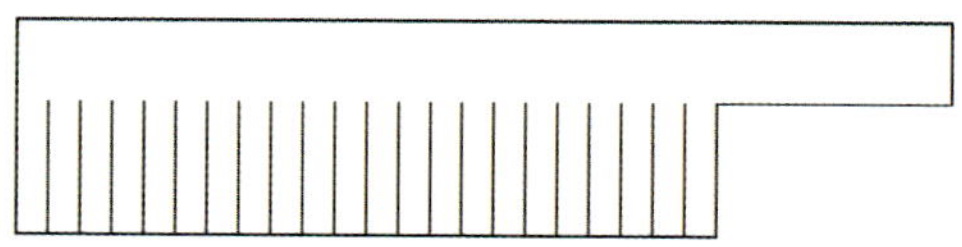

The full pattern

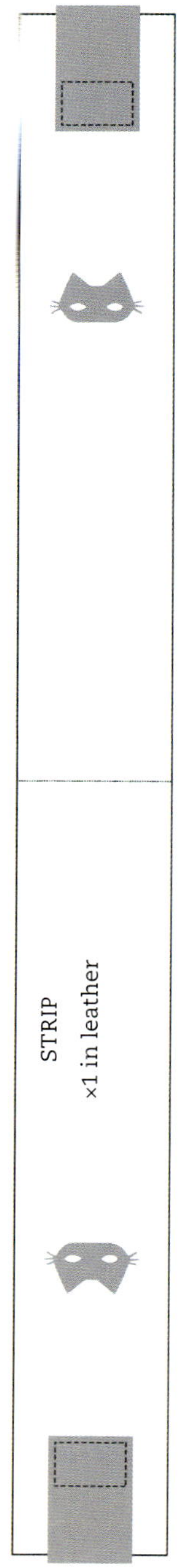

INSTRUCTIONS

Preparing the Leather

- Iron on the cat's-head motifs in the locations indicated. For this, mark the location of each head (with a small X, for example). Place the first cat on the mark, cover it with a slightly damp cloth, and press the very hot iron onto the cloth (without steam) for 20 seconds without moving the iron. Carefully remove the cloth and repeat the process, placing the cats one by one (1). Advice: it's best to do a trial run on a scrap of leather first to make sure your leather can handle the heat of the iron and to make sure the motif sticks properly to the leather.

The Lining

- Set the snap fasteners on the front lining and the main part of the bag in the locations shown (the male part of the front, the female part on the main part of the bag), placing a reinforcing piece of leather on the underside of the fabric (2). See page 13 for the instructions for setting a snap fastener.

- Place the strip of fabric on the front lining right sides together; pin the pieces together on the bottom and the sides, making sure that the sides match up, and sew them together at ⅜" from the edge (3).

- Fold back ⅜" toward the inside of the top and use the hot iron to mark the crease (4).

- Assemble the other side of the strip with the lining of the main part of the bag, right sides together, positioning the ends of the strip on the marks of the slit on the side. Stitch at ⅜" from the edge (5).

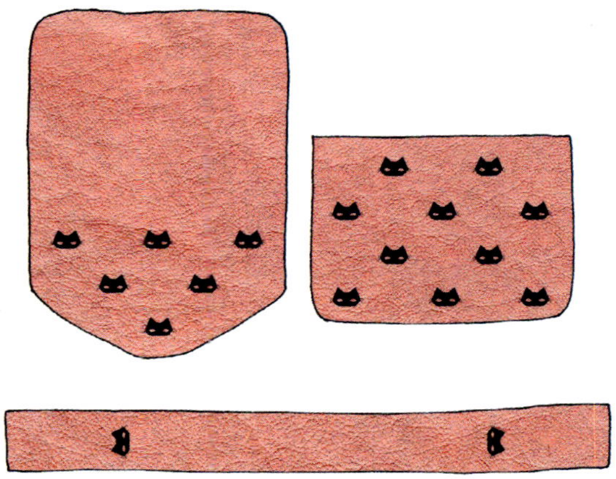

-1-

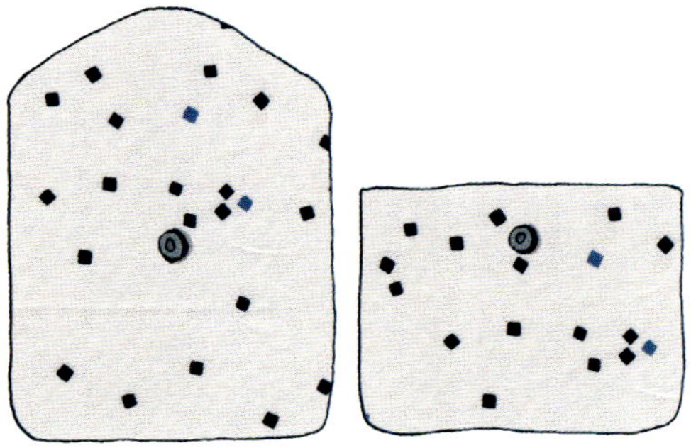

-2-

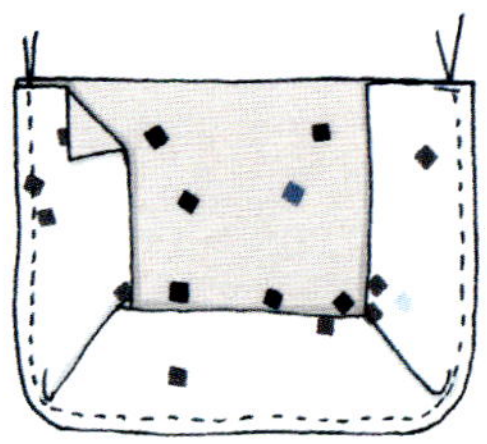

-3-

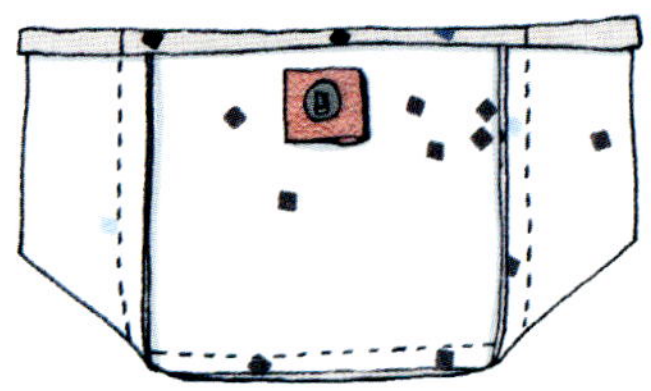

-4-

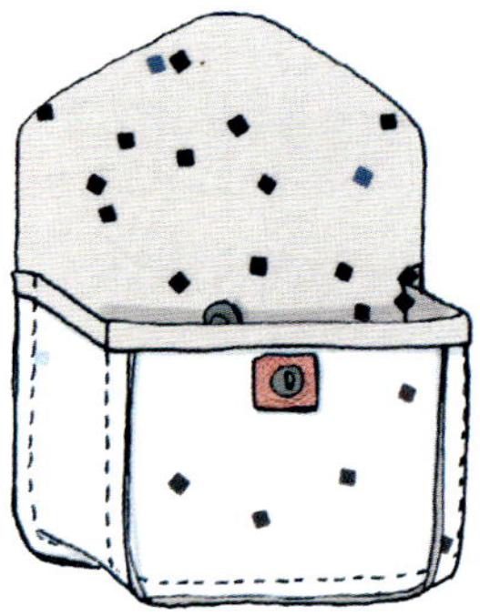

-5-

Making the Tassel and the Loops for the Shoulder Strap

- Make the tassel (see page 14) and insert the small D-ring in the doubled band (6).

- Fold the loop for the tassel in two, slip the tassel into the middle, and place the loop in the center of the flap on the inside. Stitch it in place 3/16" from the edge (7).

- Take the strips of leather for the strap loops, slip a D-ring onto each, and fold them in two, wrong sides together. Place them at each end of the leather strip in the location shown on the pattern, and stitch them in place (8).

Finishing the Bag

- Place the leather main part of the bag and the lining right sides together and stitch the flap ¼" from the edge, starting and finishing at the marks for the side slits (9).

- During this step, make sure that the tassel is correctly positioned so that you don't sew it into the seam. Clip the curved parts, cutting the slits to 1/16" from the seam. Turn the flap right side out and stitch around it at ⅛" from the edge (10).

- Assemble the leather strip on the leather front of the bag and stitch it at ¼" from the edge (making sure it is even, as you did with the lining) (11).

- Assemble the other side of the strip on the leather main part of the bag in the same way (12).

-6-

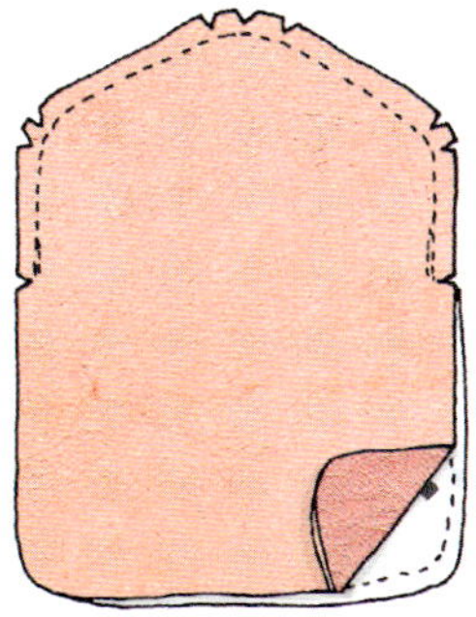

-9-

-11-

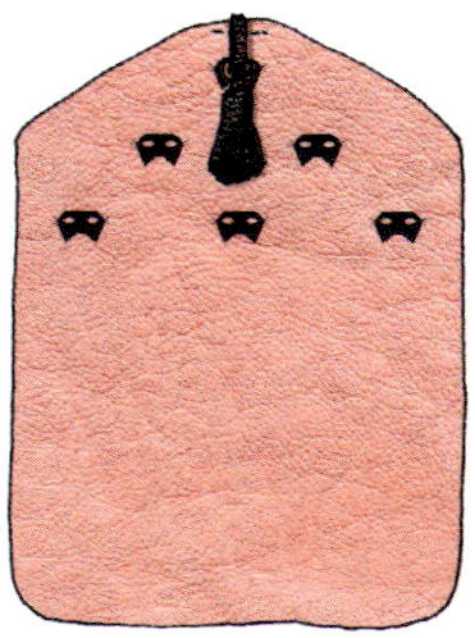

-7-

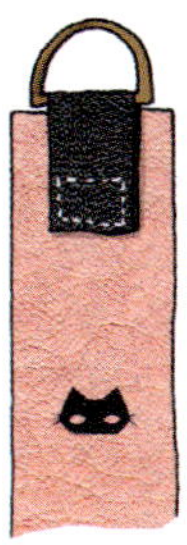

-8-

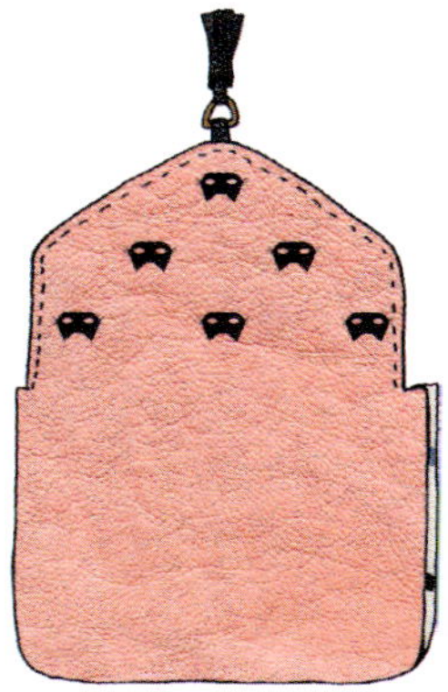

-10-

-12-

- Turn the bag right side out, slip the lining inside, and stitch around the top at ⅛" from the edge to keep it in place (13).

- Pass each end of the shoulder strap through the D-rings, fold each strap end back ⅜", and stitch each end (14).

-13-

-14-

Cat Shoulder Bag: Half Pattern

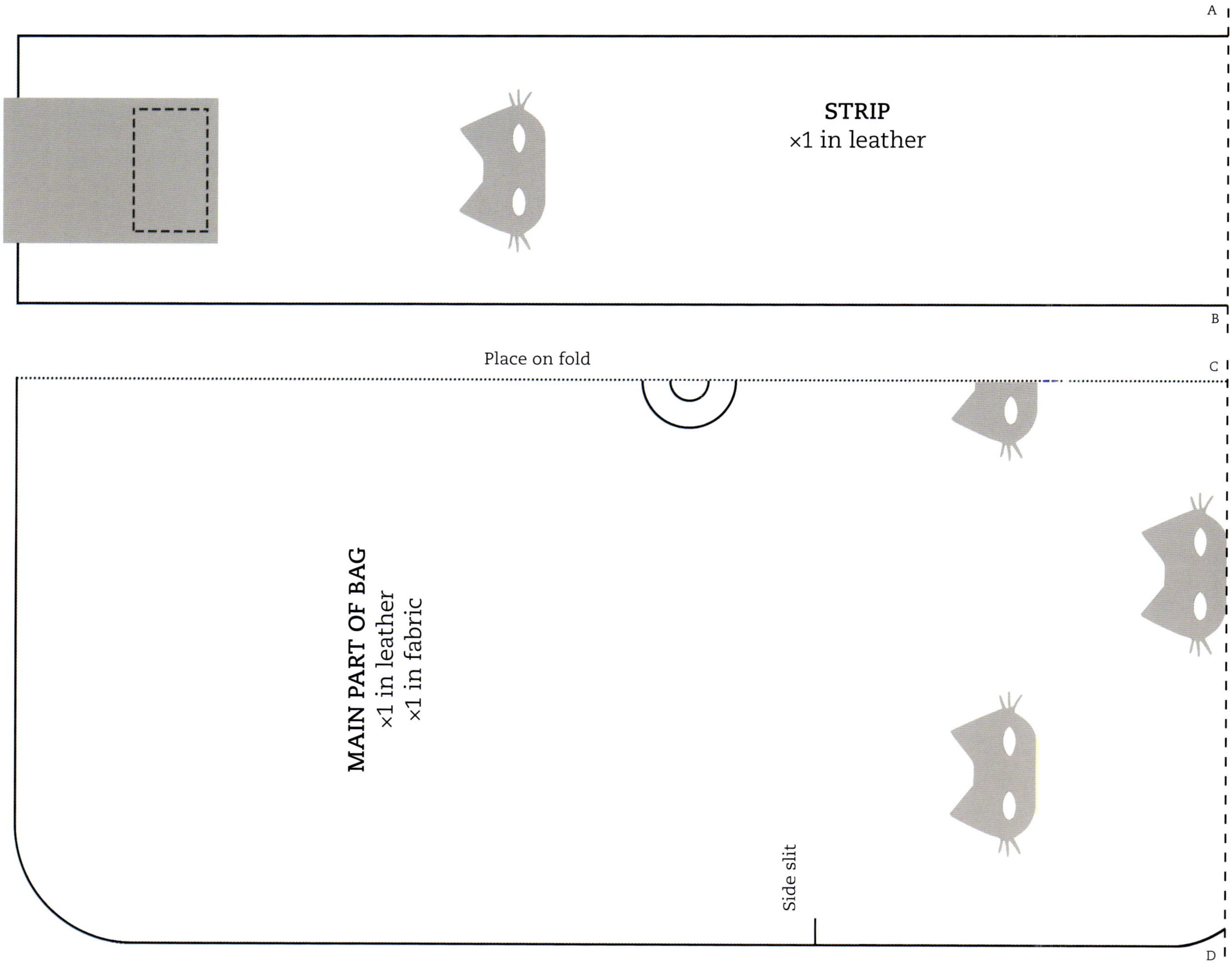

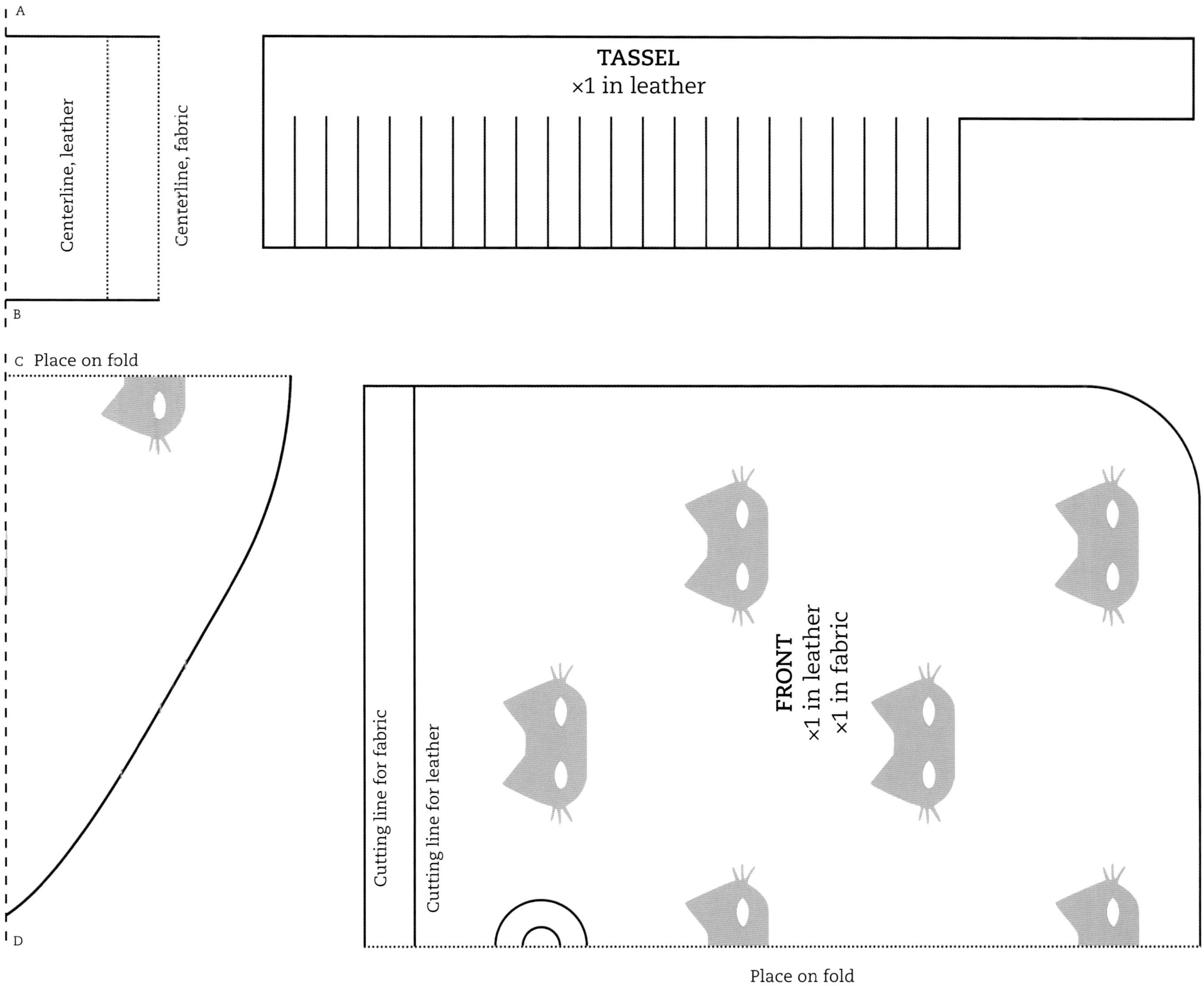
A
Centerline, leather
Centerline, fabric
B
TASSEL
×1 in leather
C Place on fold
D
FRONT
×1 in leather
×1 in fabric
Cutting line for fabric
Cutting line for leather
Place on fold

Fox Change Purse

DIFFICULTY LEVEL: ☆☆
Materials: leather sewing-machine needle, Teflon presser foot, leather glue
Recommended leather: thin, supple leather such as lambskin or goatskin
Dimension of the change purse: 4¾" × 4¾"

You'll need:

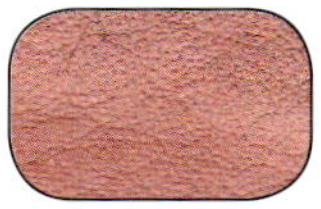
Rose blush pebbled lambskin: 6" × 11¾"

Anthracite lambskin: 6" × 4"

Silver metallic lambskin: 4" × 4"

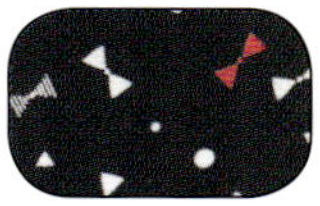
Cotton fabric (for the lining): 6" × 9¾"

1 magnetic snap fastener 11⁄16" diameter

CUTTING OUT THE FOX

- ***Main part of the change purse:*** Cut once out of the pink leather.
- ***Fox's head:*** Cut once out of the pink leather.
- ***Front bottom:*** Cut once out of the gray leather and mark the location of the slits.
- ***Front lining:*** Cut once out of the fabric.
- ***Back lining:*** Cut once out of the fabric, marking the location of the slits.
- ***Eyes and nose:*** Cut once out of the gray leather.
- ***Interior of the ears and the cheeks:*** Cut once out of the silver leather.

INSTRUCTIONS FOR THE FOX

The Lining

- Take the piece of front lining fabric. Fold back ⅜" toward the underside all along the top, marking the fold with a hot iron (clip the middle so that the curved part is even) (1).
- Place it right sides together on the back lining, pin the pieces together, and stitch the sides ⅜" from the edge (2).
- Recut the rounded part 3⁄16" from the edge and use a hot iron to fold ⅜" on all the sides toward the underside (3).

-1-

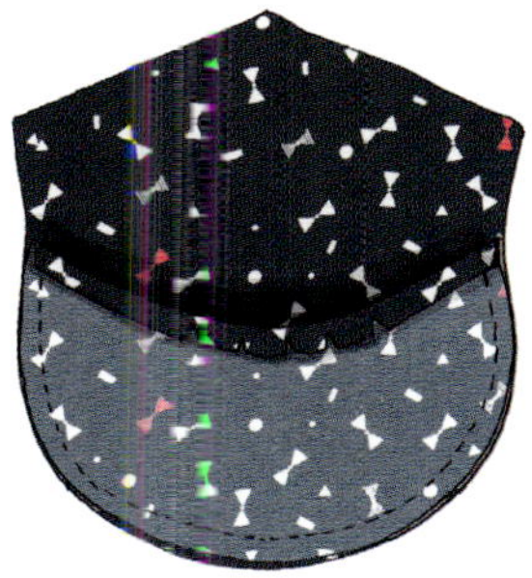
-2-

-3-

Setting the Snap Fastener

- Usie the location marks of the slits to place the snap fastener and then cut them out with small scissors or a knife. Set the two parts of the fastener, placing a leather reinforcement on the back (see page 13). The male part of the fastener is placed on the fabric, the female on the leather (4).

The Appliqués

- Take the leather shaped like a fox's head; glue on the insides of the ears, the cheeks, and the eyes with leather glue; and edgestitch them as shown in the drawing at ⅛" from the edge (5).

- Glue on the nose and edgestitch it (6).

Finishing the Change Purse

- Place the front bottom on the main part of the purse (wrong sides together following the points B) and stitch it at ⅛" from the edge (7).

- Place the fox's head, holding it in place with paper clips, then stitch the top between the points A at ⅛" from the edge (8).

- Slip the lining inside and stitch the flap and the interior part at ⅛" from the edge to join the leather and the lining (9). If the snap fastener is in the way during this part, change out the presser foot for a zipper foot, which is narrower when sewing.

-4-

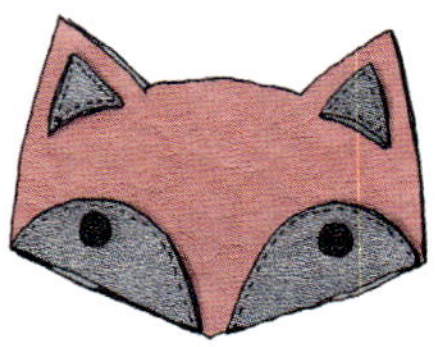

-5-

-6-

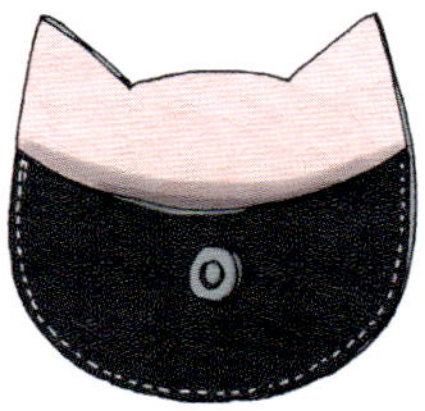

-7-

-8-

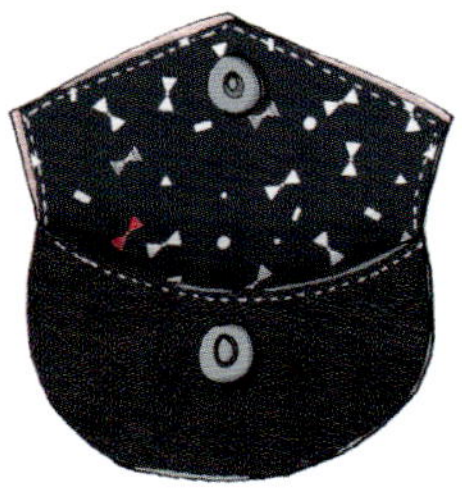

-9-

Fox Change Purse: Pattern

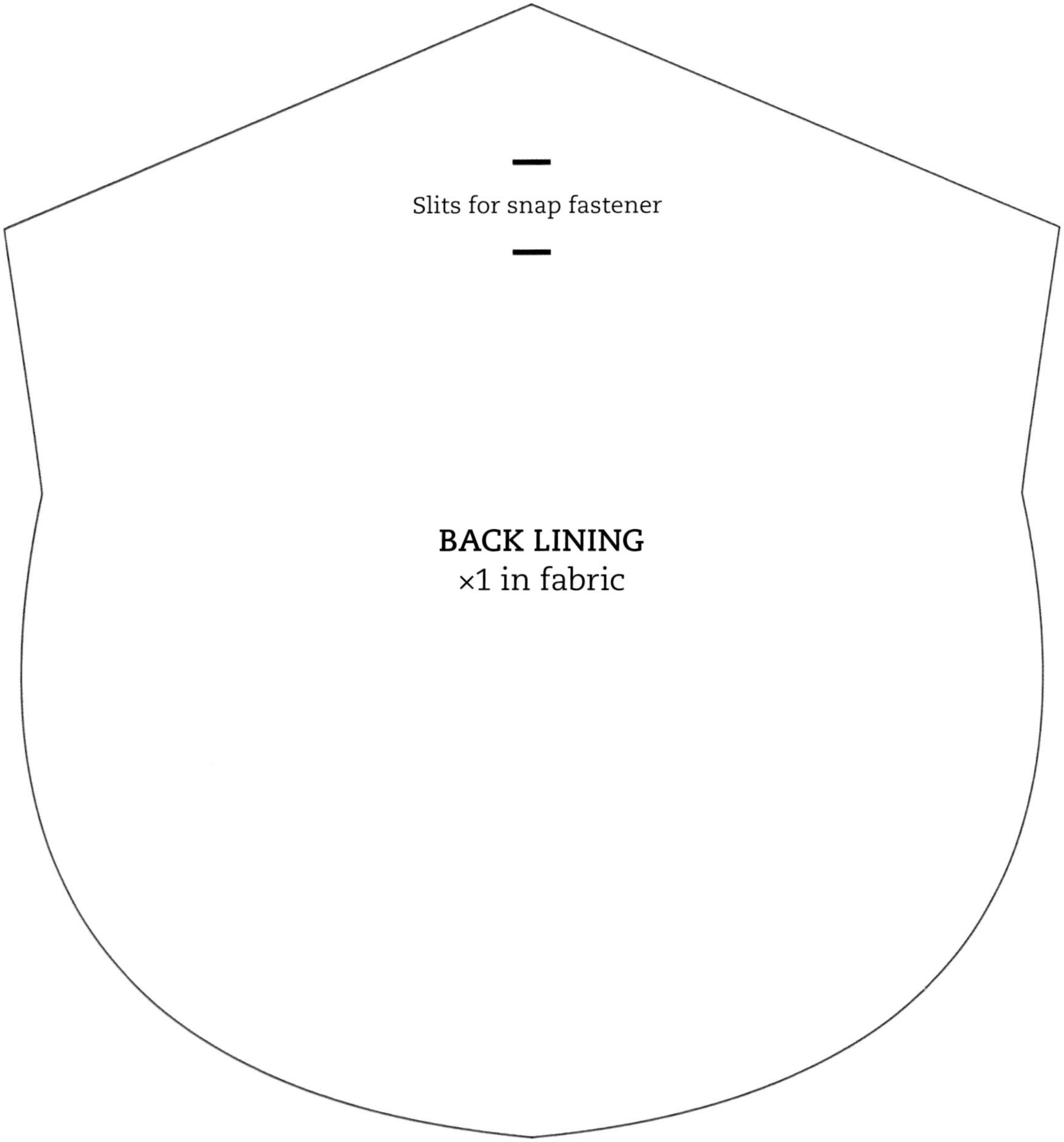

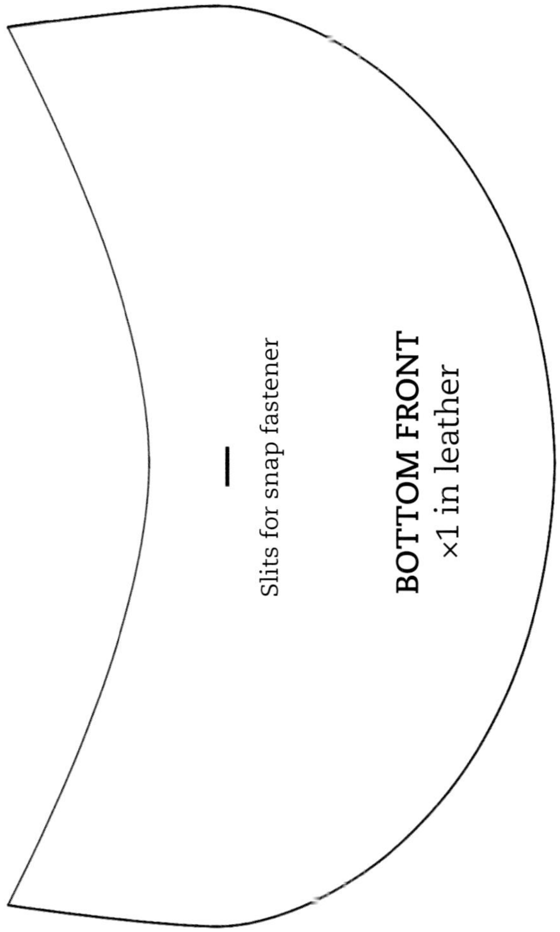

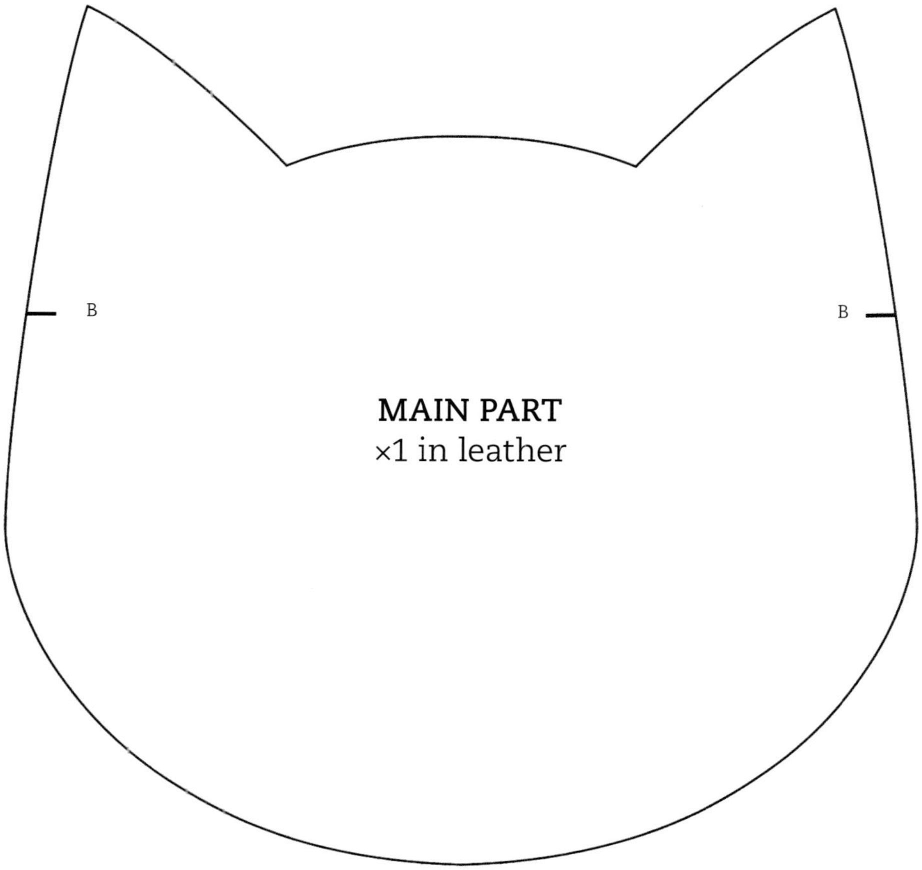
B
B
MAIN PART
×1 in leather

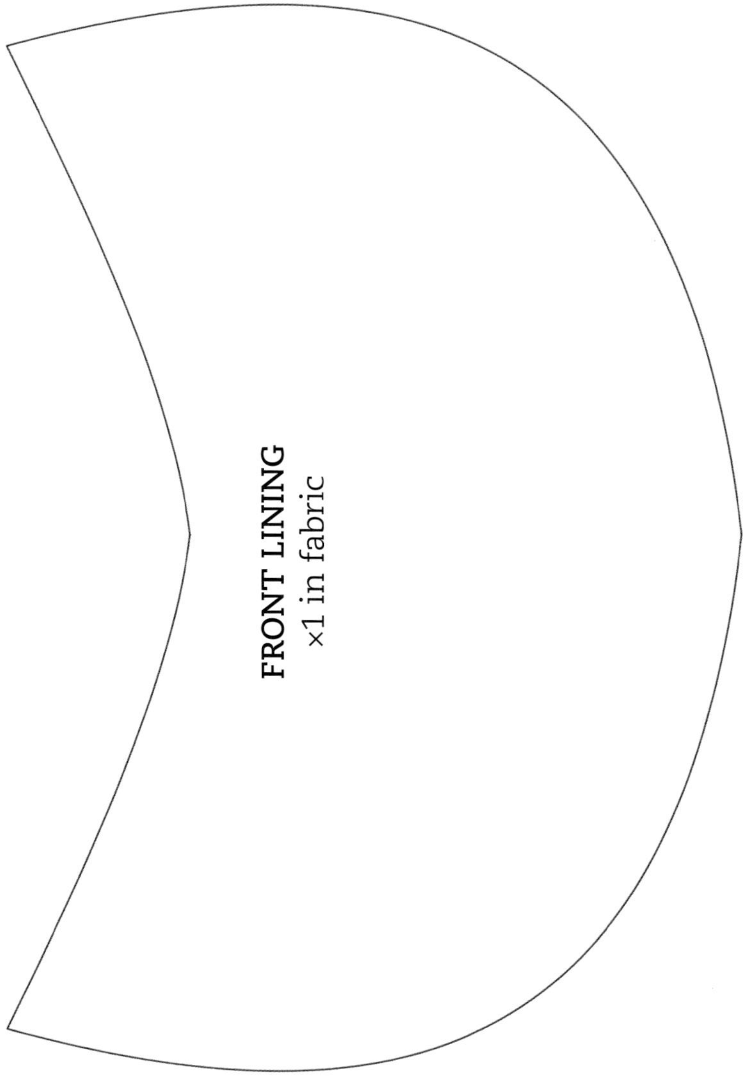
FRONT LINING
×1 in fabric

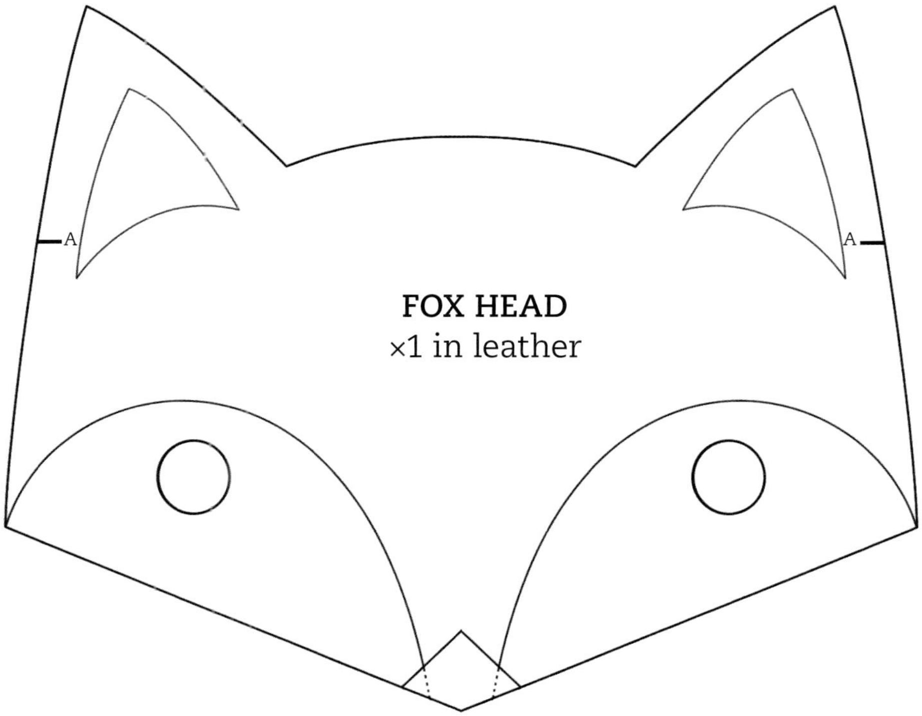
A
A
FOX HEAD
×1 in leather

Mittens

DIFFICULTY LEVEL: ☆☆
Materials: leather sewing-machine needle, Teflon presser foot, leather-marking pen
Recommended leather: fairly thin, supple leather (vegetable tanned, to avoid risking allergies in small children)
Dimensions: 2–3 years (total length 6¾"), 4–6 years (total length 7⅞")

You'll need:

Rust-colored lambskin, 3 oz. / 1 mm thick: 11¾" × 15¾"

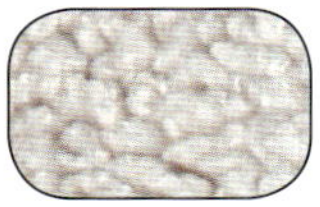

Cream-colored fake fur: 23¾" × 11¾"

CUTTING

- ***Back of hand:*** Cut twice (mirror image) out of the leather. Mark the locations indicated on the pattern on the wrong side with a leather-marking pen.
- ***Hand interior:*** Cut twice (mirror image) out of the leather. Mark the locations indicated on the pattern.
- ***Palm of hand:*** Cut twice (mirror image) out of the leather. Mark the locations indicated on the pattern.
- ***Lining:*** Cut twice (mirror image) out of the fake fur.
- ***Loops:*** Cut two bands 2" × ⅜" out of the leather.

Mittens that are so soft and comfortable that you'll feel like making an adult-size pair! The little loops on the sides allow you to join them with a cord or ribbon to avoid losing them.

INSTRUCTIONS (FOR MAKING ONE MITTEN)

- Place one palm piece on one of the hand interiors, right sides together, matching up the reference points A & A' and B & B'. Stitch from A to B 3/16" from the edge (1).

- Fold the piece so that the reference points C & C' correspond, and stitch the thumb to the reference point C, as shown in the drawing, at 1/8" from the edge (2).

- To flatten the seam along the palm, lay the margin of the seam toward the thumb and do a decorative topstitch to the starting point of the thumb's seam (3).

- Place one of the strips of leather, folded in two to form a loop, on the back of the hand between the two pattern marks. Hold it in place with masking tape (4).

- Place the hand interior on the back of the hand, wrong sides together, and stitch all the way around to point C (5).

- Raise the thumb and finish stitching from point C to the bottom of the mitten (6).

- Make the second mitten in the same way.

Lining

- Fold the fabric right sides together so that the points D & D' and E & E' match up. Sew from D to E at 3/16" from the edge (7).

- Fold the piece right sides together matching points F & F' to make the thumb. Stitch the thumb from D to F at 3/16" from the edge (8).

- Fold at point G and stitch from G to F at 3/16" from the edge (9).

- If your fake fur has a tendency to fray, use a zigzag stitch along the edge of the wrist.

Finishing the Mitten

- Slip the lining into the mitten, using a slicker to help you get the lining properly in place. If your child is at home, put the lining on her or his hand and simply slip the leather mitten over it—much easier!

- Fold the extra lining back over the base of the mitten (10).

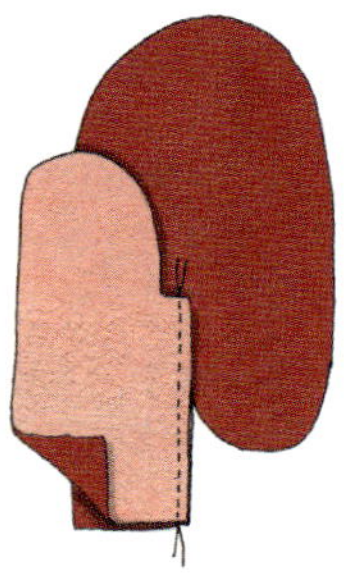
-1-

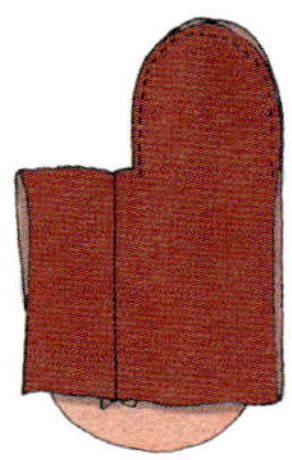
-2-

-3-

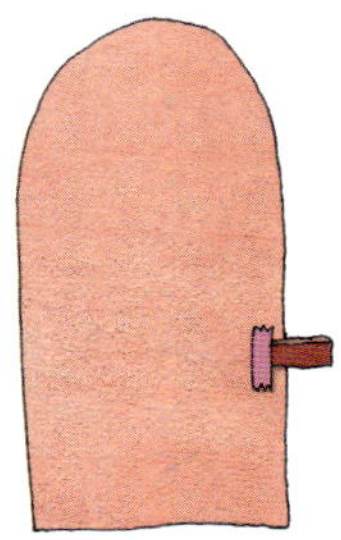
-4-

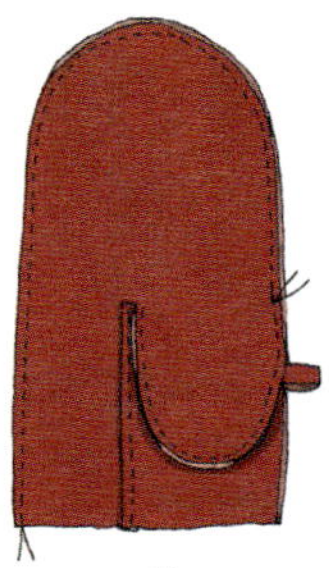
-5-

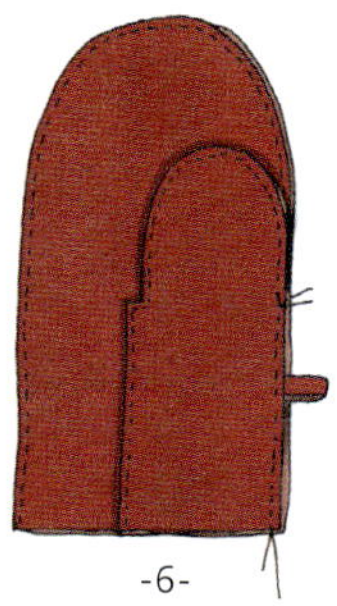
-6-

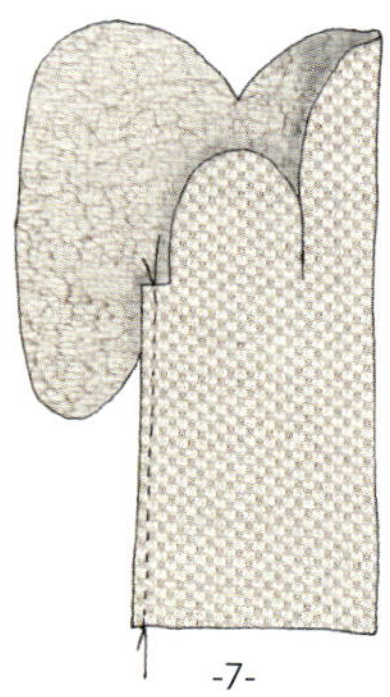
-7-

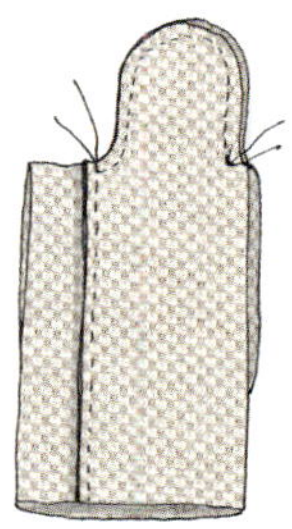
-8-

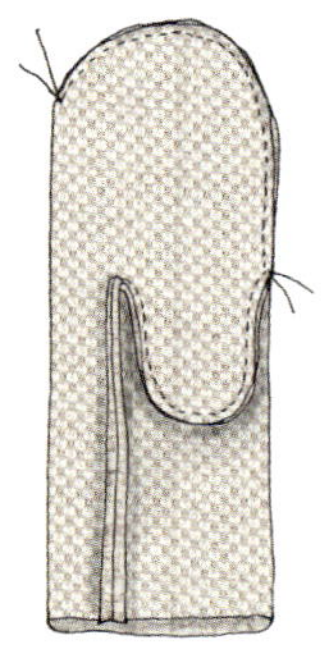
-9-

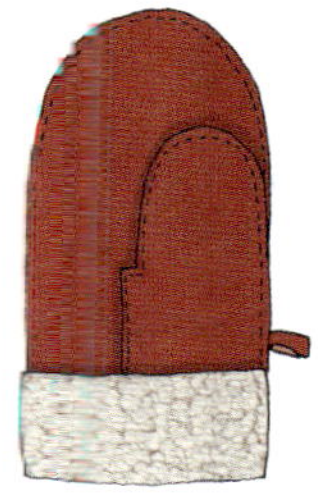
-10-

Mittens: Pattern

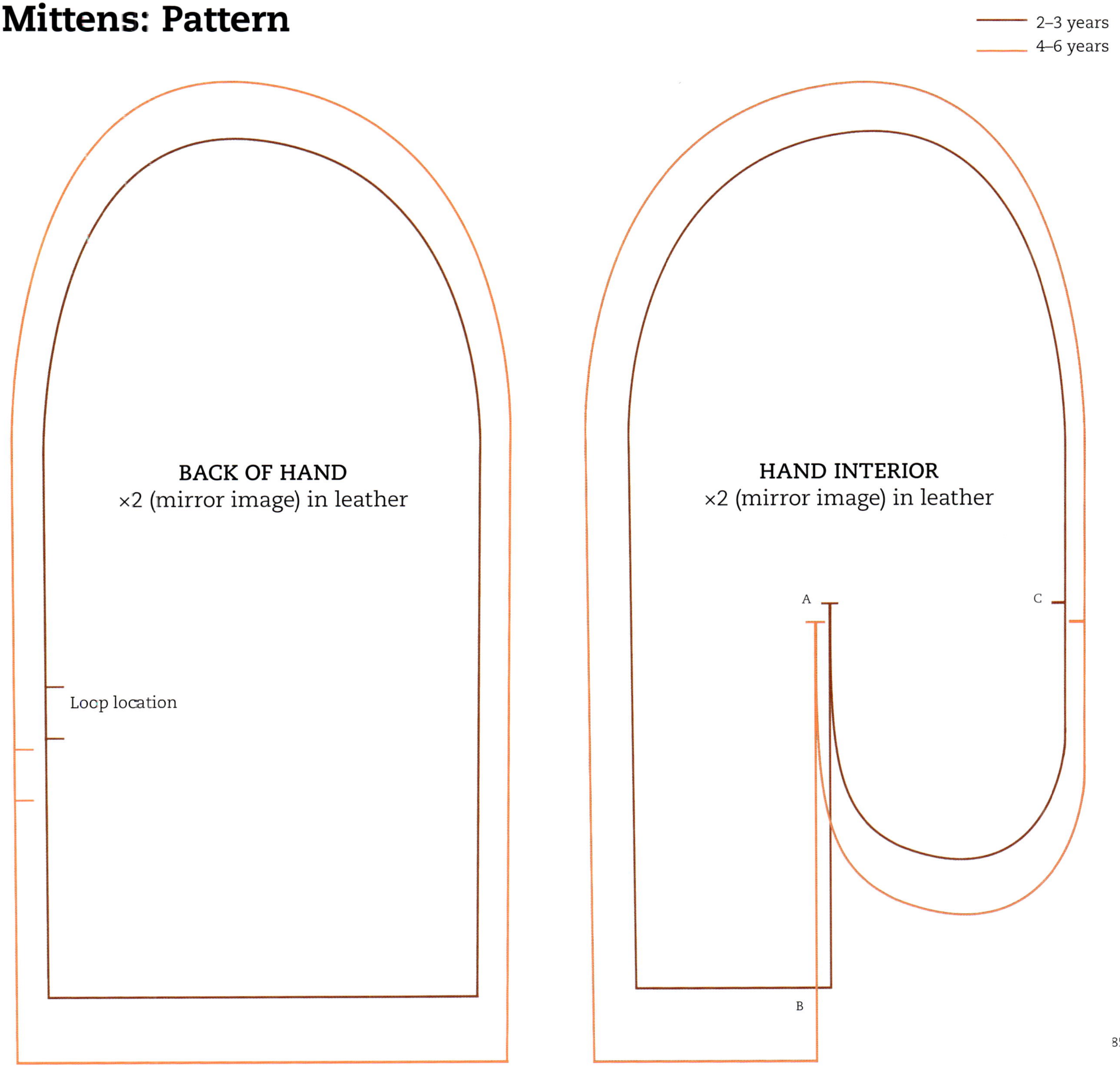

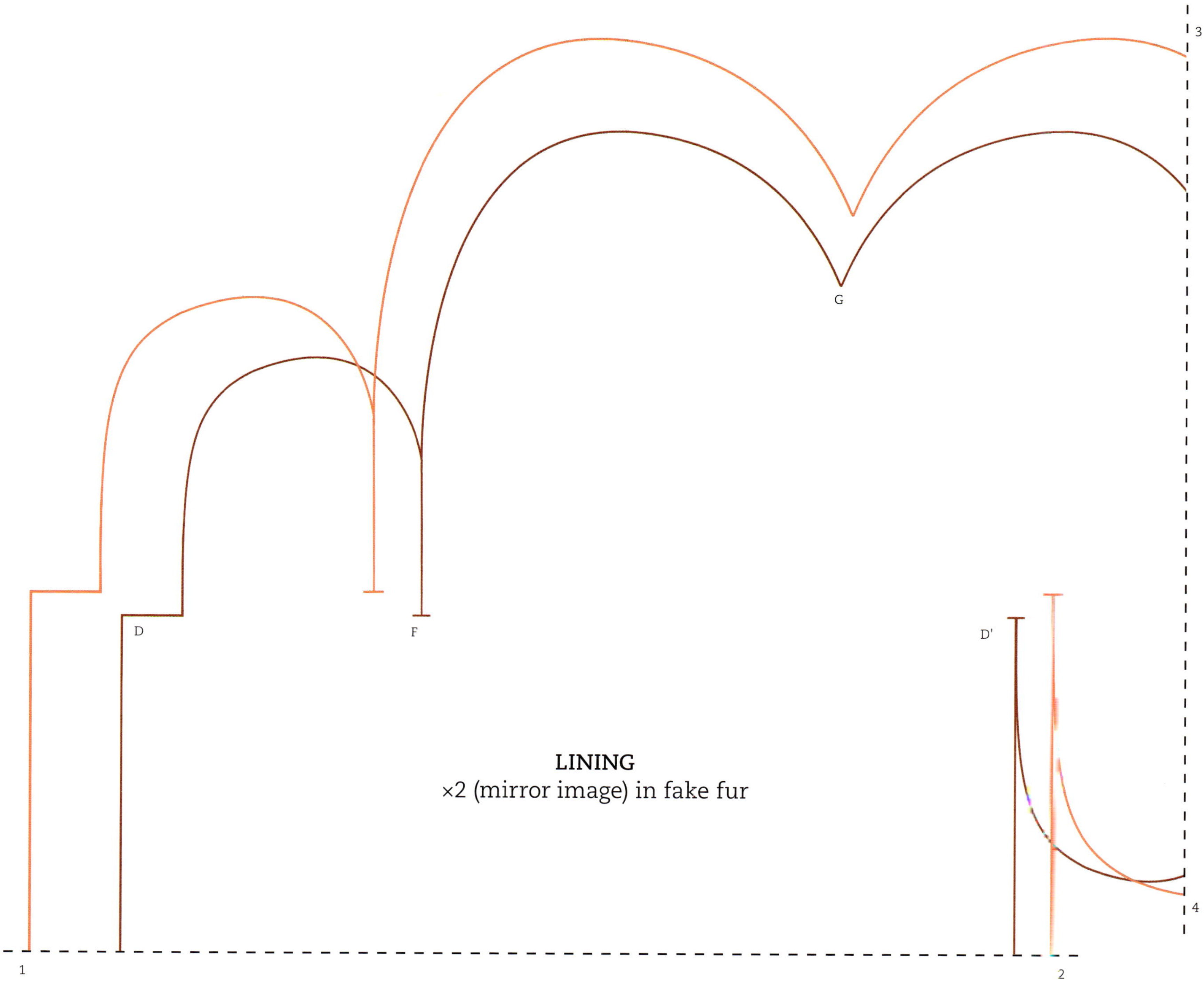
3
G
D
F
D'
LINING
×2 (mirror image) in fake fur
4
1
2

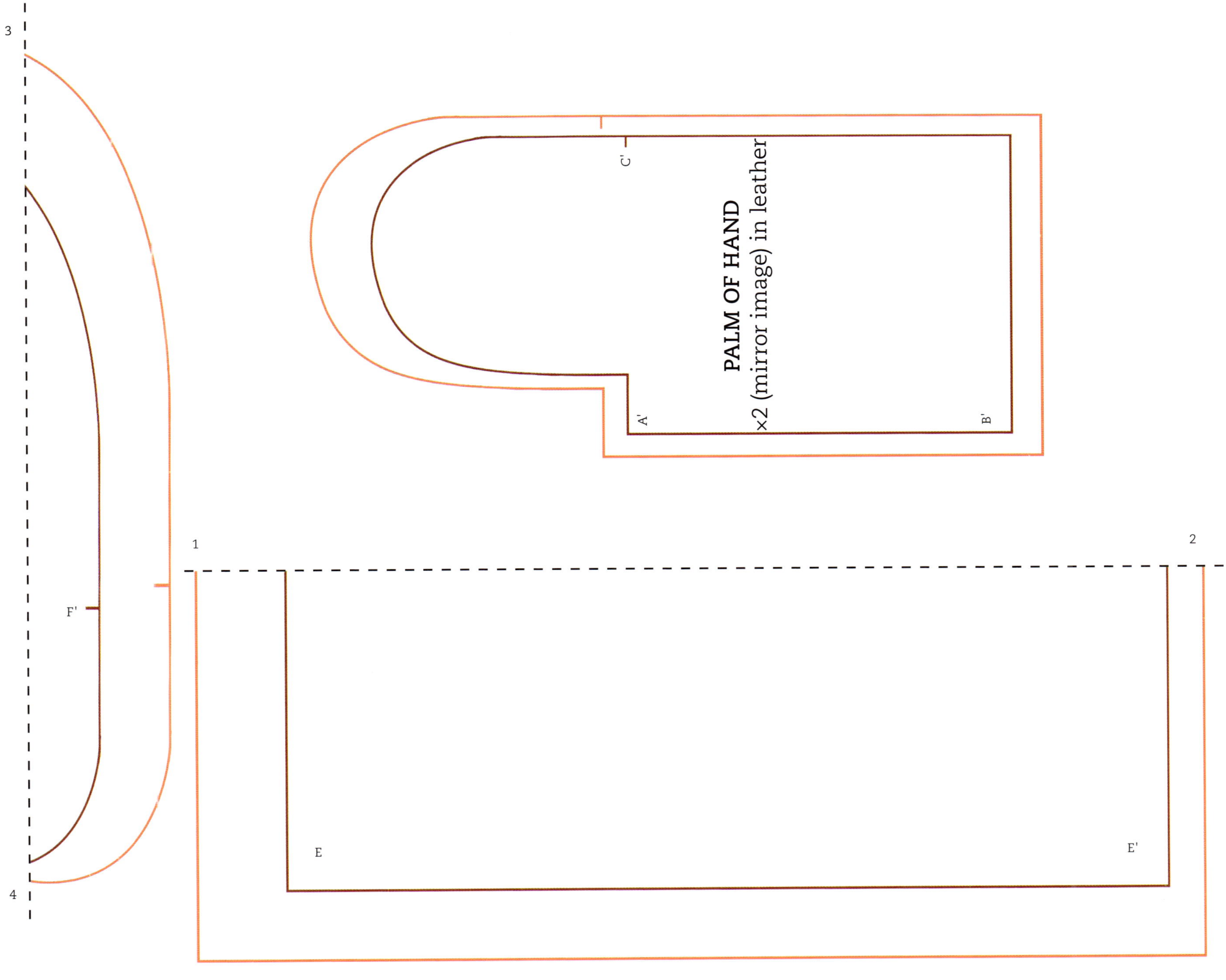
3
4
F'
PALM OF HAND
×2 (mirror image) in leather
C'
A'
B'
1
2
E
E'

Nursery School Satchel

DIFFICULTY LEVEL: ☆☆☆
Techniques: Straight stitch, setting tuck lock clasps
Materials: leather sewing-machine needle (size 16/100), Teflon presser foot, mallet, leather-marking pen, knife, punch pliers
Recommended leather: stiff leather, but not too thick
Dimensions: 11" × 9½" × 4"

You'll need:

Navy-blue suede pigskin, 3 oz. / 1.2 mm thick: 33½" × 17¾"

Metallic gold lambskin: 6½" × 11¾"

Cotton fabric: 33½" × 25¾"

Thick felt: 4" × 10¼"

Fusible interfacing for fabrics, heavyweight: 15¾" × 8"

Transparent plastic: 2¾" × 1¾"

2 tuck lock clasps, 1¼" wide

2 strap adjusters, 1¾" wide

A nursery-school-sized satchel that's a lovely gift for your child's first school adventure!

LOIRE FL.
Cl de la Sauldre
Bourgogne
CHER R.
Cl du Nivernais
Cl latéral
SAONE
DOUBS R.
Cx du Berry
à la Loire
VIENNE R.
Cl du Centre
SAONE R.
RHÔNE FL.
LÉGENDE
Échelle 1/750.000
Cl du Midi
LOIRE FL.
CHER R.
THE ART OF INSTRUCTION

CUTTING

- ***Shoulder straps:*** Cut two bands 4¾" × 13¾" and two bands 15¾" × 4" out of the fabric. Cut two bands 2" × 13" out of the felt. Cut two bands 15" × 3⅛" out of the interfacing.
- ***Lining:*** Cut two rectangles 9½" × 11" out of the fabric (front and back), two rectangles 9½" × 4¾" (sides), and one rectangle 11" × 4¾" (bottom).
- ***Pocket:*** Cut the pattern once out of the gold leather, marking the locations indicated on the pattern.
- ***Front of the satchel:*** Cut a rectangle 9" × 11" out of the navy-blue leather.
- ***Back of the satchel:*** Cut a rectangle 9" × 11" out of the navy-blue leather.
- ***Sides of the satchel:*** Cut two rectangles 9" × 4¾" out of the navy-blue leather.
- ***Bottom of the satchel:*** Cut a rectangle 1" × 4¾" out of the navy-blue rectangle.
- ***Flap:*** Cut the pattern once out of the navy-blue leather and once out of the fabric.
- ***Name label holder:*** Cut the pattern once out of the gold leather and cut a rectangle 2¾" × 1¾" out of the transparent plastic.
- ***Tongues:*** Cut the pattern twice out of the navy-blue leather.
- ***Handle:*** Cut a rectangle 8¼" × 1⅜" out of the navy-blue leather and another rectangle 9" × 1¼" out of the fabric.

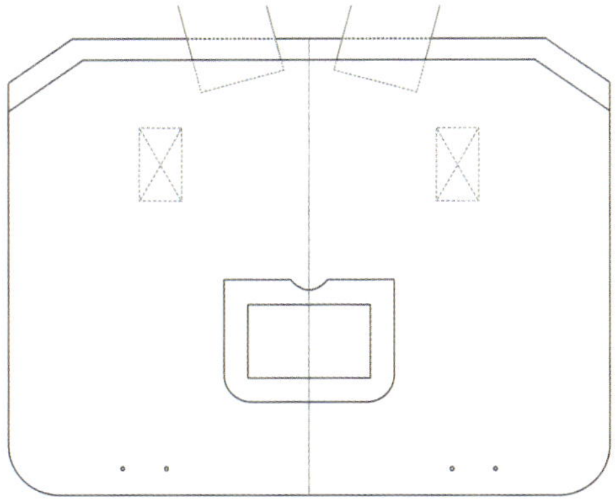

The full pattern

INSTRUCTIONS

Shoulder Straps

- Take the two rectangles 15¾" × 4" and iron on the interfacing bands on the underside, leaving a margin of ⅜" on all the sides, then fold them lengthwise right sides together. Stitch the long side and one short side at ⅜" from the edge (1).
- Clip the corners, turn it right side out, iron it, and sew a decorative edgestitch at ⅛" from the edge (2).

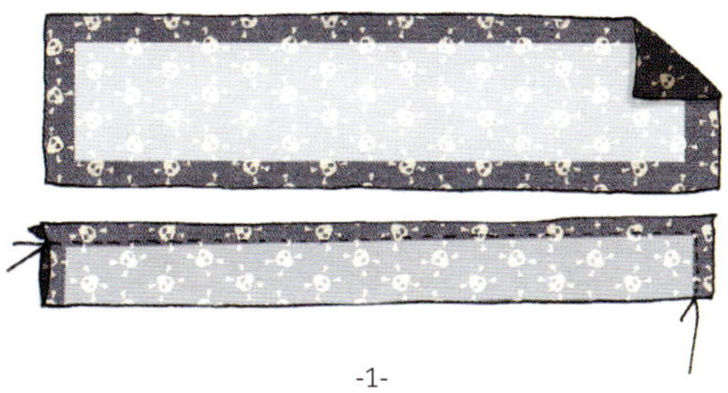

-1-

- Place the straps on the leather back of the satchel on the underside, as shown in the drawing; stitch them in place (3).
- Take the two bands 4¾" × 13¾" (shoulder straps) and fold them in two lengthwise; stitch the three sides at ⅜" from the edge, leaving a 3" opening along the long side (4). Clip the corners, turn it right side out, and iron it.

-2-

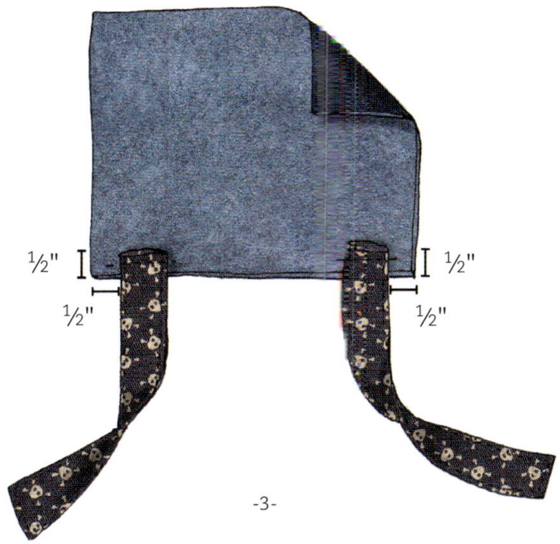

-3-

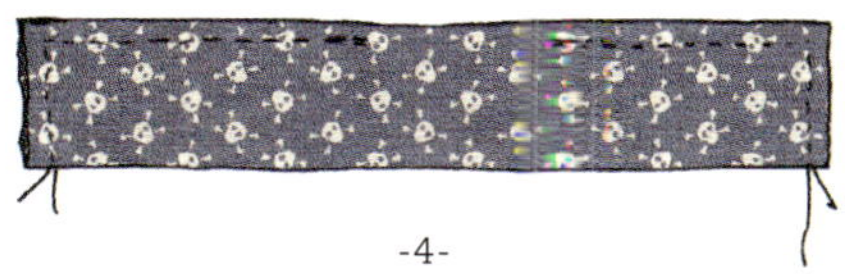

-4-

- Insert the band of felt through the opening (5). Place it correctly and close the opening with blind stitch.

- Along each shoulder strap, sew rows of straight stitch ⅜" apart (6).

- Sew the shoulder straps to the strap adjusters, folding back ¾" and attaching with a straight stitch (7).

The Lining

- Place the fabric rectangle for the bottom of the satchel on one of the large fabric rectangles, right sides together; stitch at ⅜" from the edge, starting and finishing the seam at ⅜" from the two ends (don't forget to backstitch at the beginning and at the end) (8).

- Place the two fabric rectangles for the sides and stitch them on, leaving ⅜" at the bottom of the seam (9).

- Now stitch the sides and the bottom together, leaving ⅜" at the beginning and at the end of the seam (10).

- Add on the second large rectangle in the same way to complete the lining.

- Use a hot iron to fold a crease ⅜" toward the underside all the way around the top of the lining (11).

-5-

-6-

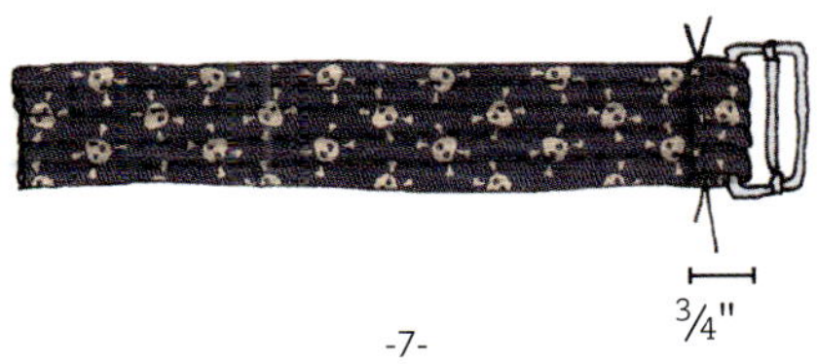

-7-

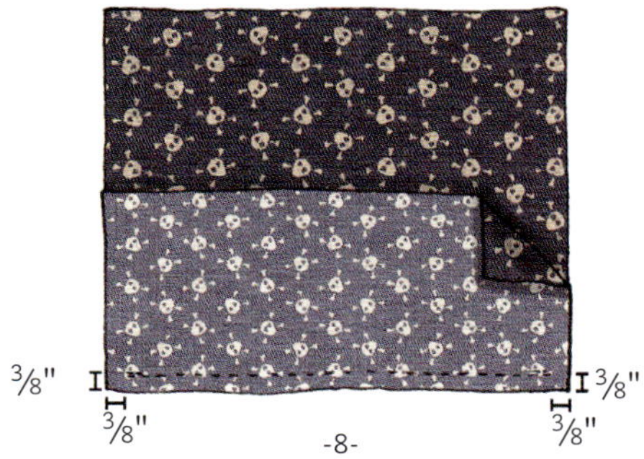

-8-

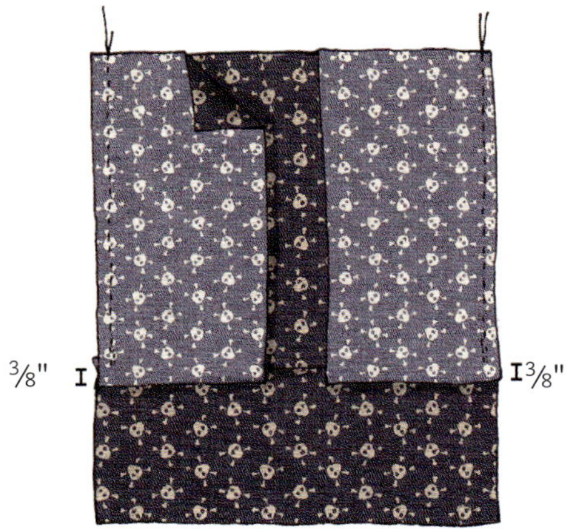

-9-

-10-

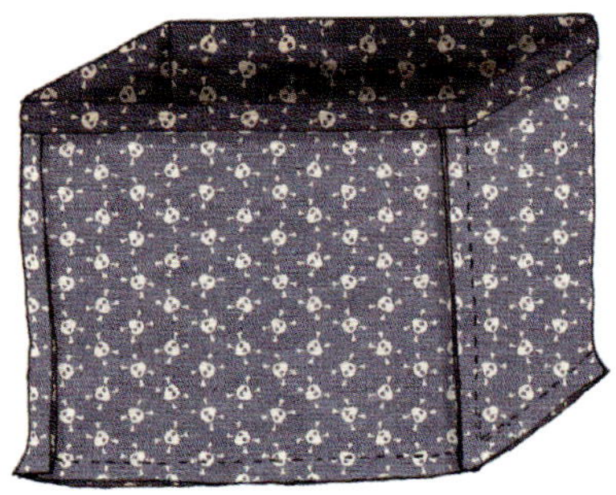

-11-

The Pocket

- Place the female parts of the fasteners on the pocket in the locations shown on the pattern (12). See page 12 for how to set them.

- Install the needle and the Teflon presser foot onto your machine. Stitch the pocket onto the front of the satchel (see the pattern for the location) at ⅛" from the edge, doing a reinforcing stitch at the top of each side (13).

The Handle

- Use a hot iron to fold under ⅜" on all sides of the cotton rectangle (14).

- Place the leather rectangle over it, wrong sides together. Stitch at ⅛" from the edge (15).

- Fold the handle in two lengthwise, leather on the outside. Stitch the two thicknesses for a length of 1½" between the two location marks, at ⅛" from the edge (16).

The Name Label Holder

- Place the transparent rectangle on the underside of the label holder; hold it in place with masking tape and stitch all around the rectangle at ⅛" from the edge (17).

- Stitch the label holder onto the leather flap at the location marked on the pattern (18).

The Flap

- On the top of the flap's lining, use a hot iron to fold under ⅜" as shown in the drawing (19).

- Place the lining on the leather flap right sides together. Stitch the three sides at ⅜" from the edge (20).

- Clip the rounded corners and turn it right side out.

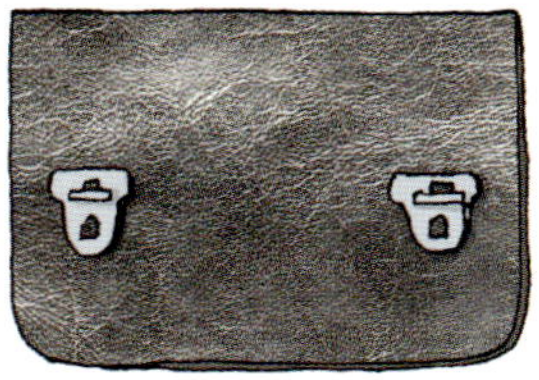

-12-

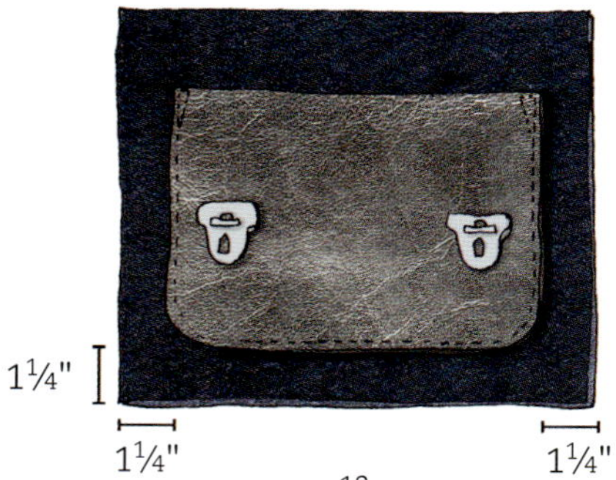

-13-

-14-

-15-

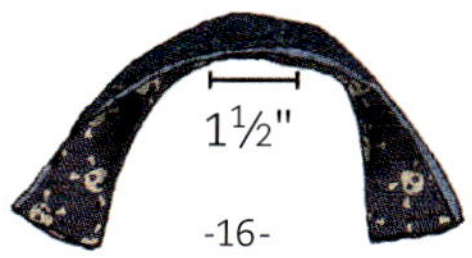

-16-

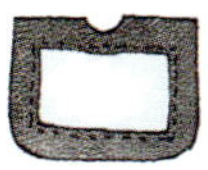

-17-

-18-

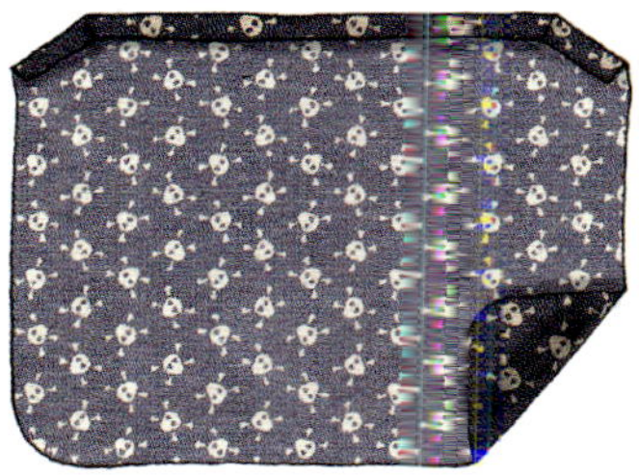

-19-

-20-

- Place the shoulder straps in the location marked on the pattern, between the leather and the lining. Hold them in place by pinning them to the lining. Stitch all around the flap at ⅛" from the edge (21).

- Use the punch pliers to make ⅛" holes at the locations marked for the tuck lock clasps. Make holes in the tongues too.

- Set the tuck lock clasps (see page 12). Stitch the handle to the flap at the location marked on the pattern (22).

- Stitch the flap onto the back of the satchel at ⅛" from the edge of the flap (23).

Finishing the Satchel

- Assemble the front and the bottom of the satchel wrong sides together, stitching ¼" from the edge, starting and finishing the seam ¼" from the edge (24).

- Assemble the sides and the back in the same way as you did for the lining (making sure that the straps are correctly placed and are solidly sewn into the seam of the bottom of the satchel).

- Slip the lining inside the satchel and stitch the four sides one after the other at ⅛" from the edge (25).

- Join the straps to the strap adjusters (26).

-21-

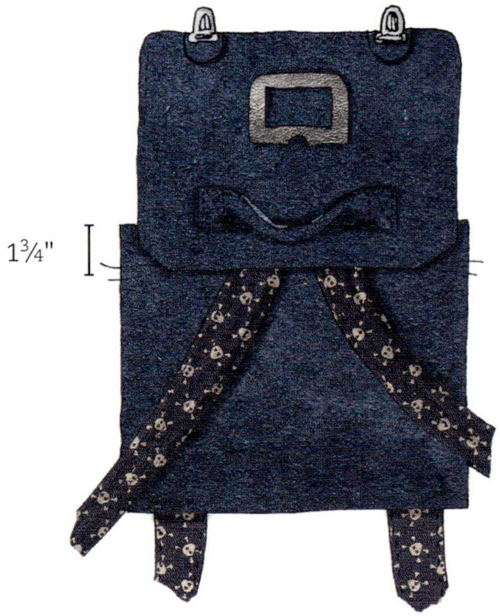

-23-

-22-

-24-

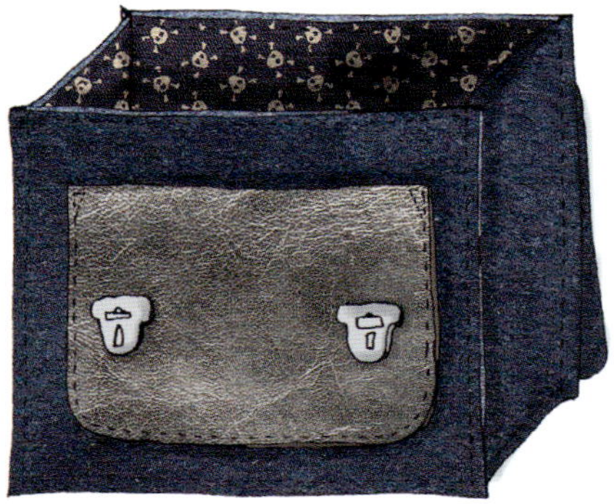

-25-

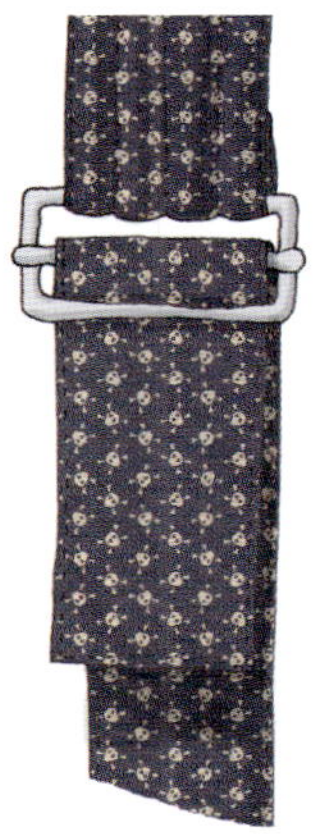

-26-

Nursery School Satchel: Pattern

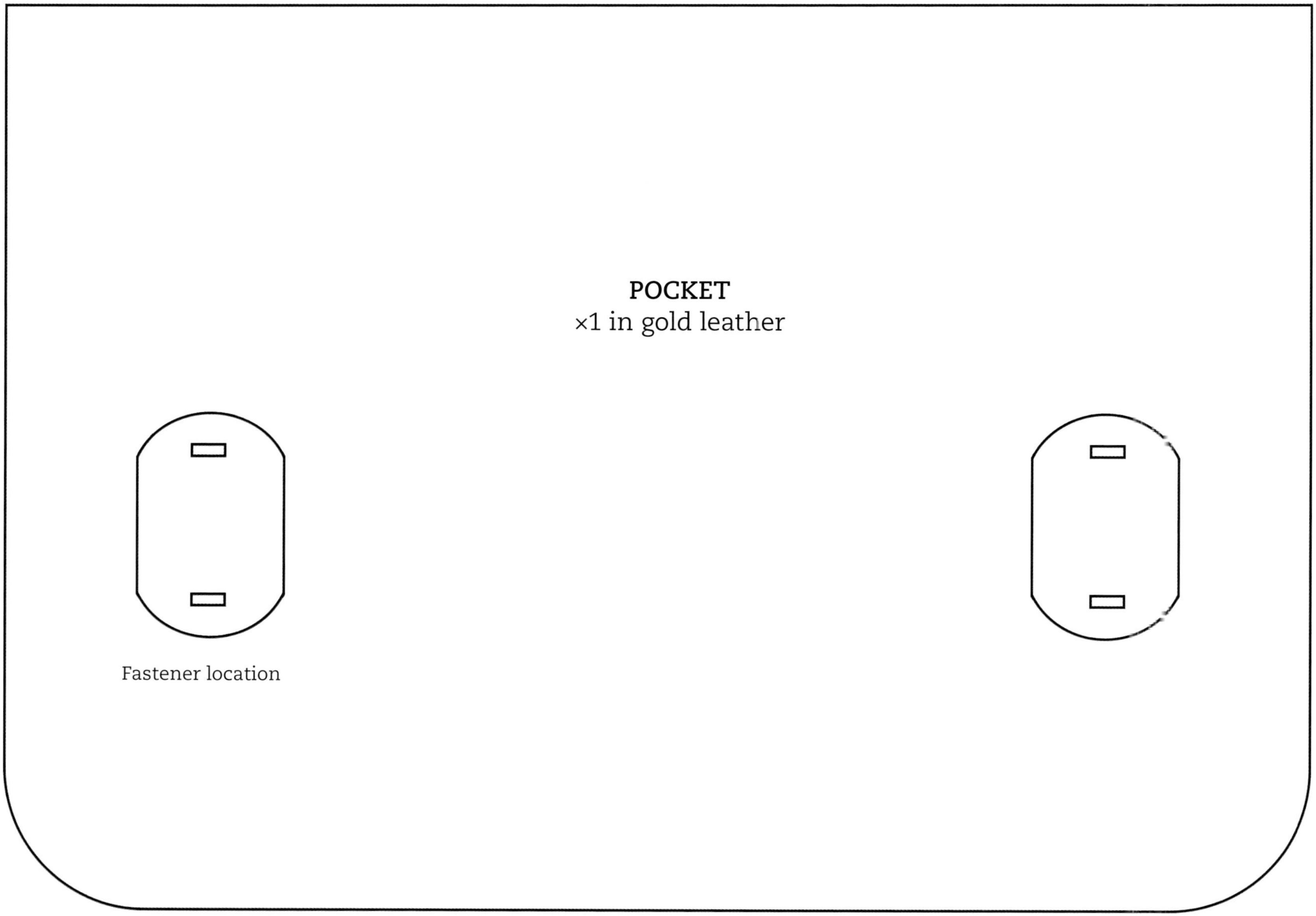

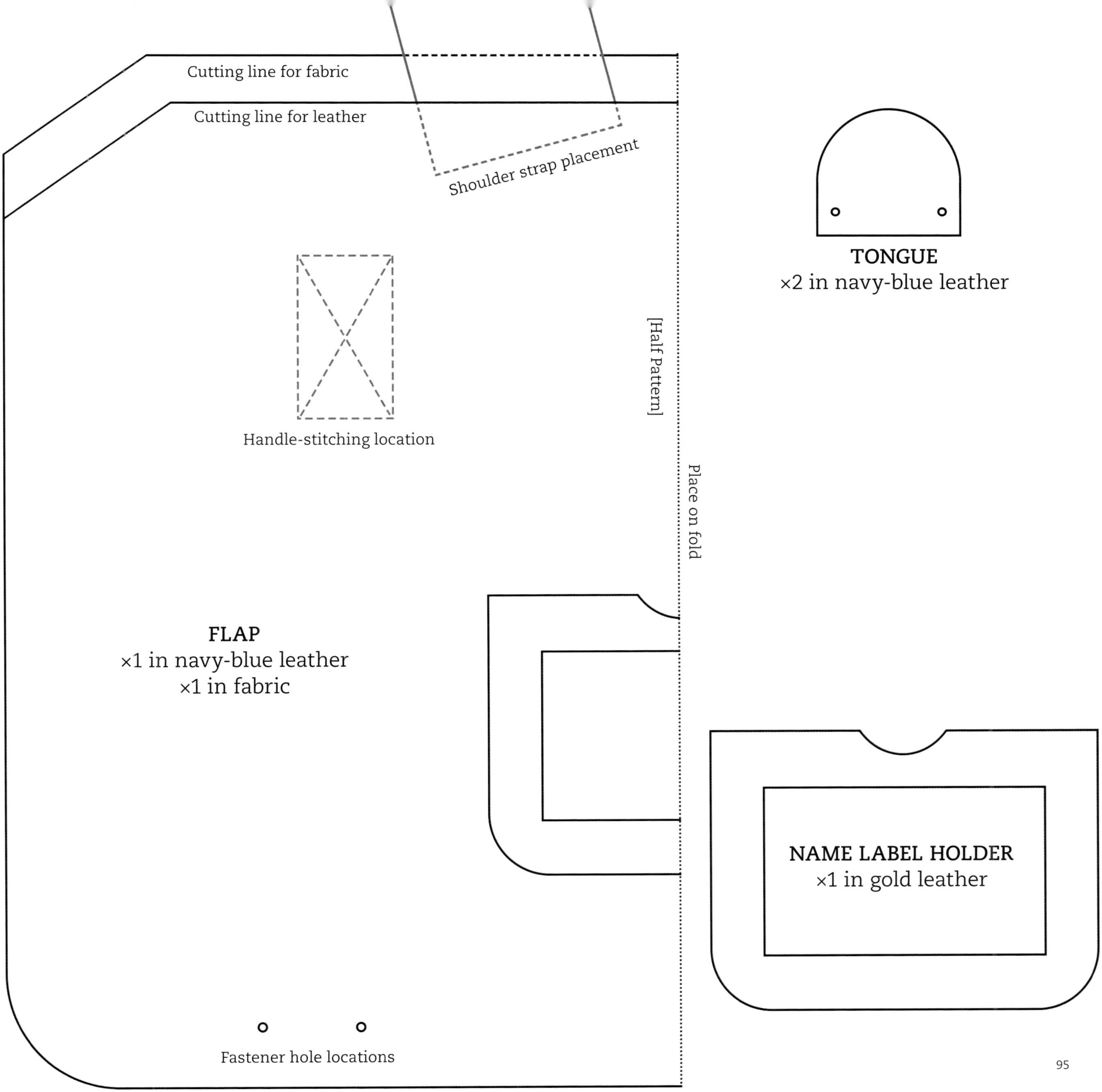
Cutting line for fabric
Cutting line for leather
Shoulder strap placement
Handle-stitching location
[Half Pattern]
Place on fold
FLAP
×1 in navy-blue leather
×1 in fabric
Fastener hole locations
TONGUE
×2 in navy-blue leather
NAME LABEL HOLDER
×1 in gold leather

Mélanie Voituriez is passionate about creative decoration and embellishment. She worked in textile design before becoming a freelance artist and illustrator. Based near Paris, she enjoys creating the little things that make life sweeter. Visit her blog at www.melanievoituriez.com.